The Bulldog Guide to Business Divorce

By Terrance W. Moore

Published 2021 by Bulldog Guides, Minneapolis, MN

Every effort has been made to obtain permissions for material quoted throughout the book. If any required acknowledgements have been omitted, or any rights overlooked, it is unintentional. Please notify the publisher of any omission, and it will be rectified in future editions. While I am a bulldog lawyer, I am not yet your bulldog lawyer. Nothing in this book should be considered legal advice.

Library of Congress Control Number: 2021910564

Cover design by: Andrew Cadle

Interior design and formatting by The Guerrilla Group

Printed in the United States

ISBN: 978-1-7368906-0-8

**This book is dedicated to
all business partners.**

What they're saying about The Bulldog Guide to Business Divorce

"Terry has worked on my rights deals for many years. I would trust no one else. He is one of those rare individuals who understands that good strategy is built upon empathy and respect. Always insightful, tenacious and fair, and unfailingly creative, he is the man whose counsel you want when seeking to understand how best to work with your business partners." ~ Kent Nerbern, Author: *Neither Wolf Nor Dog; The Girl who Sang to Buffalo;* and many others

"A much-needed resource in the complicated world of business partnerships. Builds a stunningly logical path toward preventing business angst and regret." ~ Maribeth Vander Weele, President, Vander Weele Group, Author: *The Joy of Job, An Investigator's Perspective on the Most Righteous Man on Earth*

"At Compassionate Geek, we are always looking for ways to add value for our business clients. The Bulldog Guide to Business Divorce will help strengthen any partnership and the stories are great!" ~Don Crawley, Author, *The Compassionate Geek*

"It's a whole new ball game--going from craft knowledge to going into business for yourself. The Bulldog Guide to Business Divorce should be on the shelf of everyone who is considering moving from entrepreneur to business owner. ~ Carla Cross, Real Estate Company Owner and Business Consultant; Author, *Launching Right in Real Estate; Up and Running in 90 Days*, and many others.

Table of Contents

What Makes a Bulldog? ....**xv**

Introduction...**xix**

    These Stories are True...xx

    What is a Business Bulldog?.................................xxi

    Disclaimers xxi

SECTION I...**1**

Chapter 1: Build a Successful Partnership **3**

A Foundation of Loyalty, Honesty and Openness.................**3**

What is a Partner's Fiduciary Duty? **5**

    The Duty of Loyalty.. 6

    The Duty of Honesty 9

    The Duty of Openness 12

The Rest of the Story...**13**

Chapter 2: Good Founding Documents Make

        Good Partners **15**

Control Agreements **18**

Buy-Sell Agreements...**20**

Operating Agreements and Bylaws 26

The Rest of the Story 26

Chapter 3: Set Reasonable Expectations with
Good Planning 29

Agree Early on the Purpose of the Business 36

Decide Early on How to Resolve Disputes 37

Good Planning Comes from Strong Communications 39

Communication Must be Full and Open 39

The Rest of the Story 43

Chapter 4: Choose Your Partners Carefully 45

Pick Partners You Trust 48

Pick Partners with Complementary Skills 50

Pick a Partner with the Same Business Attitude 50

Mountain Climbers 51

Freedom Fighters 51

Craftspeople 51

The Rest of the Story 54

SECTION II 55

Chapter 5: Habits 57

Poor Communication 60

Revisionism 62

Self-Destructive Behavior 64

Experimentation 65

Regular use 66

Table of Contents

Problem or risky use 66

Dependence 66

Addiction 67

Bad Habits Can Sometimes Be Fixed 67

The Rest of the Story 68

Chapter 6: Traits 69

Warning Signs 70

Finances 70

Bad at the Job 72

Cheating 73

Irresponsible behavior 74

The Rest of the Story 77

Chapter 7: Differing Values and Vision 79

Differing Values and Vision 82

Values 83

Vision 84

Mission Statements and Vision Statements 86

The Rest of the Story 88

Chapter 8: Red Flags 89

Unilateral Action 91

Using Company Credit Cards for Personal Expenses 93

Lying or Hiding Information 94

Breakdown in Communication 95

The Rest of the Story 96

SECTION III **99**

Chapter 9: When It's Time to Go **101**

**What to do when it's time to separate from
your partners.** **104**

    Understand your Rights and Obligations 105

    Creating Your War Plan...105

    Decide on your Attitude 105

Understand Every Party's BATNA............................**107**

    What will happen to your *partner* if no agreement
    is reached? 108

    What will happen to *you* if no agreement
    is reached? 108

    Can you take action to change either BATNA?...............109

Prepare Budgets for both Time and Expense **110**

Set Your Goals **111**

The Rest of the Story..**114**

Chapter 10: Timelines and Tactics **117**

Phase One - Months 1-3: Planning and Setup......................**119**

**Phase Two - Months 4-6: Negotiation and
Commencement of Litigation** **120**

    The First Move...120

    Capital Call 120

    Deadlock 121

    Adverse Actions 122

    Valuation and Offer...122

Table of Contents

Closing Without Litigation 123

Fundamentals of Closing..123

Seasoning..123

The Golden Silence 124

Split-the-Difference Close 125

False Withdrawal: The Doorknob Close...........................127

Two Futures Close.. 128

Closing against Separation Anxiety..................................... 129

What if your partner surprises you? 132

**Phase Three – Months 6-18: Litigation,
Mediation and Trial.. 134**

The Rest of the Story.. 136

Chapter 11: Getting the Business Ready for a Divorce........... 139

Obtain a Professional Valuation of the Business 141

Get Your Finances in Order 142

Get Your Agreements in Order 144

Keeping Your Important Customers and Suppliers 144

Keeping Your Important Employees 146

Get Your Operations in Order..148

The Rest of the Story.. 149

Chapter 12: Finding Money to Buy out Your Partner............. 153

Payments Over Time..155

Traditional Bank Financing 155

High-risk Bank Loans...157

Asset-based Lenders 158

Factoring 159

Hard Money Lenders 160

Investors 161

Friends and Family 161

Venture Capital/Private Equity 162

The Rest of the Story **163**

About the Author 165

Bring Your Bulldog **165**

What Makes a Bulldog?

1. Integrity: Be Honest with everyone-including yourself

2. Tenacity: Go after what you want and don't stop until you have it.

3. Courage: Take on the hard challenges and big projects.

4. Ferocity: When you attack, attack with everything you have.

5. Loyalty: Be true to your allies

6. Pugnacity: Never shy away from a necessary fight.

7. Judgment: Choose your actions deliberately

Forward

L ove is blind.

Like a marriage, most business partnerships start out all sunshine and roses. There's a mutual attraction. A growing company attracts capital, or a piece of land attracts a developer, or an inventor attracts an entrepreneur. Each partner contributes something different, and they're stronger together. There's a he-can-do-no-wrong honeymoon that sometimes lasts for decades.

Many business partnerships end in divorce. Something drives a wedge between the partners; differences in values or goals, a shift in the business climate, or problems with money or health. A business built on trust and respect falls into conflict and chaos. Unraveling these relationships can be simple and amicable, or messy and contentious.

And just like a domestic divorce, you need an advocate who understands the dynamics, the conflict, and the law.

In this book, Terry raises the many questions partners should ask *before* merging their interests. He calls out the warning signs of a partnership going sour, and gives you a solid war plan to exit the relationship, while keeping custody of your assets.

It should be a must-read for anyone taking on a partner, and certainly for anyone who feels it may be time to part ways.

— Orvel Ray Wilson – co-author, "Guerrilla Selling"

Introduction

I n 2020, as COVID ravaged the world and wreaked havoc on small businesses, I began to look for a way I could help business owners weather the storm. An informal survey of clients revealed that business owners were looking for a read-able, straightforward guide to help them understand challenges common to all types of business partnerships. The result was *The Bulldog Guide to Business Divorce.*

Business partnerships come in many forms, including corpora-tions, limited liability companies and joint ventures, in addition to the various forms of partnerships. For our purposes, we refer to all of these business entities as "partnerships," and all co-owners as "partners."

This guide is divided into three parts that follow the life cycle of business partnerships and business partners.

The first section guides you in choosing your partners and forming your agreements to minimize chances of trouble later. Except for your spouse and family, your business partner will be the most important relationship in your life. This section explains the legal duties all partners owe each other; the agreements all partners should agree to at the very start; how to plan to reach your business goals; and the right way to pick your business partners.

The second section describes the characteristics you should look for in *choosing* your partner, and the warning signs that your partnership might be in trouble. This section discusses problems to look for and how to handle them, including certain habits, traits and values of your partners that may change over time. This section ends with a discussion of Red Flags, signs of serious trouble on the horizon.

The third section discusses the various pleasant and unpleasant ways that business partnerships end. This section discusses financing, preparing for sale or succession, and what to do if your partnership is headed for a business divorce.

The Bulldog Guide to Business Divorce is intended to be useful to business owners during the entire life cycle of the business. It will not teach a cobbler to make better shoes, but it can help her run a stronger business partnership.

These Stories are True

The principles discussed are demonstrated by the true story that opens each chapter. Some of these stories are from my cases and some are from published court records. The details have been changed to disguise the real players, but the stories are all based on true events. We break away to explain the principles involved. Don't worry though. Each chapter ends by finishing the story, explaining what happened and how the principles apply.

What is a Business Bulldog?

In business, you sometimes need to take on beasts that are bigger, badder and brawnier than you. The Bulldog is the breed you want to navigate delicate, complicated and important legal challenges of business.

Bulldogs were originally bred to fight bears and bulls for the entertainment of 19th Century England. This made bulldogs clever, creative and stubborn. When these bloody battles were outlawed, bulldogs were bred to be affectionate and kind. The result is a breed that is resolute, tenacious and courageous. Bulldogs are known to have a calm dignity about them. They are not out to pick a fight, but once it starts, bulldogs never quit.

That's what you need to successfully play in the tall grass of business partnerships.

Disclaimers

I am a bulldog lawyer, but I am not yet *your* bulldog lawyer. Nothing in this book should be treated as a substitute for legal advice that applies to your specific situation. Your agreements and state law may be different than those in the case stories. Never hesitate to call a lawyer to discuss your own situation. Like most lawyers, I am always happy to take calls from business people who find themselves in need of advice.

Section I

Chapter 1:
Build a Successful Partnership

A Foundation of Loyalty, Honesty and Openness

The story of Gordon Blesi and Melvin Evans is not unusual.[1] Close friends since college, they decided to go into business together as the Blesi-Evans Company. At that point, neither knew that one of them would eventually use misrepresentation, intimidation, and threats to force the other out of the company, or that a judge would require they be separated because of the severe acrimony. Their story is a cautionary tale for all good friends who want to become business partners.

The first two years after college were eventful for Blesi and Evans. They both took jobs with the Albert C. Price Company, a manufacturer's representative for HVAC and plumbing supplies. Mr. Price fired Blesi after six months, for reasons lost to time. Shortly thereafter, Evans found a new partner, Lloyd Steirly, and they bought the company from Price. This opened the door for

---

1   *Evans v. Blesi*, 345 N.W.2d 775 (Minn. Ct. App. 1984).

Blesi's return. Steirly and Evans sold Blesi eighteen percent of their stock, and they each kept 41 percent.

About a year later, Evans and Blesi combined their interests to vote Steirly out as President and Director. The two acquired Steirly's shares, with Evans lending Blesi funds so they could be 50/50 partners. Evans and Blesi formalized their relationship with a Shareholder's Control Agreement (a type of partnership agreement that we will discuss in depth in Chapter 2). The business was a success. The partners operated the business for 22 years, sharing equal salaries, management duties, and benefits.

At about the 22-year mark, Evans developed health problems, including high blood pressure, anxiety, and tremors in his hands. Blesi claimed this illness caused Evans to make several costly mistakes. Blesi confronted Evans about these performance issues, and threatened to dissolve the company.

Nothing was resolved, and the issues escalated, until one day Blesi exploded. In his tantrum, he demanded that Evans give up his shares. Blesi threatened to form a separate company and take away all the accounts. Evans finally agreed to give Blesi majority control by selling him one share of stock. Remarkably, Evans and Blesi returned to working equal hours, drawing equal pay and benefits, and equally sharing the day-to-day management, just as in the halcyon days. Blesi still contended that Evans continued to make costly mistakes, but all was well for five more years.

At that point, Blesi consulted an attorney about the "problem" with Evans. Blesi wanted Evans out. Blesi's internal thoughts are lost to time, but it's easy to imagine that he believed Evans was so ill that he was no longer providing the same value to the business, and could be replaced. Perhaps Blesi envisioned owning the entire company, using his client relationships, and keeping all the profits. He had already threatened as much.

Blesi's attorney advised him to offer Evans two options: resign, or be removed. The law firm prepared two sets of documents: one set for Evan's resignation; the other to remove Evans as an officer, director and employee. In either case, Blesi would be left with total control of the company.

Evans found himself looking at two bleak futures, and steeled himself for an ugly meeting with Blesi. He needed to find a third choice.

A Bulldog Lawyer would insist that you always be loyal, open, and honest with your business partners. This is the *fiduciary duty* partners owe each other. This duty is imposed by law. More important is that this is the best way to create an effective business partnership.

What is a Partner's Fiduciary Duty?

Under the law, business partners owe each other the fiduciary duty to act in an "honest, fair, and reasonable manner in the operation of the corporation and the reasonable expectations of all shareholders."[2] The relationship among shareholders in closely

---

2   Minnesota Statutes § 302A.751, subd. 3a provides that in determining whether to grant equitable relief, courts shall "take into consideration the duty which all shareholders in a closely held corporation owe one another to act in an honest, fair, and reasonable manner in the operation of the corporation and the reasonable expectations of all shareholders."

held corporations owe each other the same duty.[3] In a fiduciary relationship, including business partners, "the law imposes upon them the highest standards of integrity and good faith in their dealings with each other."[4]

This means partners must be loyal, open and honest with each other. Everyone would agree that business partners should treat each other in an honest, fair and reasonable manner, if that can be defined. Following this rule is not always easy, which is why you need to be a bulldog. Bulldogs address difficult situations head on. If you have a problem with your partner, it's best to confront it.

At first blush, it appears Blesi violated this rule when Evans became sick, and Blesi took steps to remove him. The Golden Rule doesn't always apply because it's subjective. For example, the Golden Rule would be satisfied if Blesi had expected Evans to do the same thing if Blesi were sick.

The law provides partners an objective standard to determine their actions. The three fiduciary responsibilities of all partners are the duties of **loyalty, honesty,** and **openness**.

The Duty of Loyalty

Partners owe each other a duty of loyalty. They must put the best interest of the company above their own personal, or other business interests. Efforts to compete, or making secret profits from side dealings are typical examples of disloyalty.

---

3   *Evans v. Blesi*, 345 N.W.2d 775, 779 (Minn. Ct. App. 1984); Westland Capitol Corp. v. Lucht Eng'g Inc., 308 N.W.2d 709, 712 (Minn. 1981).

4   *Prince v. Sonnesyn*, 222 Minn. 528, 535, 25 N.W.2d 468, 472 (1946).

Under the *Corporate Opportunity Doctrine*, partners may not secretly divert or take advantage of business opportunities for their own personal profit. The duty of loyalty mandates that, "the best interest of the corporation and its shareholders takes precedence over any interest possessed by a director, officer or controlling shareholder, and *not* shared by the stockholders generally."[5] Partners, "are not permitted to use their position of trust and confidence to further their private interests."[6]

The duty of loyalty arises in many situations, but two are most prominent. The duty of loyalty is violated most often by a partner who usurps a corporate opportunity, or by a partner who is guilty of self-dealing.

If an opportunity arises for the business, a shareholder cannot seize it for himself. The duty of loyalty requires this opportunity to be first presented to the company. The definition of "opportunity" is technical, but you can think of it as an opportunity that the business would normally undertake.[7] If, in such circumstances, the interests of the corporation are betrayed, the corporation may claim *all* of the benefits of the transaction for itself.[8]

---

5   *Cede & Co. v. Technicolor, Inc.*, 634 A.2d 345, 361 (Del. 1993).

6   *Guth v. Loft, Inc.*, 5 A.2d 503, 510 (Del. 1939).

7   *Du Pont v. Du Pont et al.*, D.C., 242 F. 98, reversed on facts, 3 Cir., 256 F. 129; *Beatty v. Guggenheim Exploration Co.*, 225 N.Y. 380, 122 N.E. 378; *Irving Trust Co. v. Deutsch*, 2 Cir., 73 F.2d 121, certiorari denied; *Biddle v. Irving Trust Co.*, 294 U.S. 708, 55 S.Ct. 405, 79 L.Ed. 1243; *Bailey v. Jacobs, supra*; *Beaudette et al. v. Graham et al.*, 267 Mass. 7, 165 N.E. 671; *McKey v. Swenson*, 232 Mich. 505, 205 N.W. 583.

8   Ibid.

A partner also violates the duty of loyalty if he engages in self-dealing; that is, putting the company into a business relationship with another company in which he has an interest. When a business leases land from a partner, or buys supplies from a company in which the partner has an interest, the partner is self-dealing. Such relationships themselves are not prohibited, but they must be handled carefully. This includes *full disclosure* of the arrangement, and *approval* by the company, *without* the vote of the self-dealing partner. In total, the deal itself must satisfy the *Entire Fairness Test*. This means it must be fair to the company in *all* respects. The requirement of fairness is unflinching in its demand that where one stands on both sides of a transaction, he has the burden of establishing its entire fairness.[9]

The Entire Fairness Test has two aspects: *Fair Dealing* and *Fair Pricing*. The Bulldog examines questions of *when* the transaction was timed, how it was initiated, structured, negotiated, disclosed to the directors, and how the approvals of the partners were obtained. Examination of Fair Dealing is fact-intensive. Fair Pricing is shorthand for the financial aspects of the transaction, including all relevant factors, including assets, market value, earnings, future prospects, and any other elements that affect the value of a company's stock. All aspects of the transactions must be examined as a whole. The partner violates his duty of loyalty even if the whole deal was disclosed and approved, but the financial outcome was unfair to the business. Likewise, if the deal was fair but done in *secret*, it will fail the Entire Fairness Test.[10]

---

9   *Weinberger v. UOP, Inc.*, 457 A.2d 701 (Del. 1983).

10 Ibid.

Ask yourself these two questions to determine if you are in compliance with the fiduciary duty of loyalty. When considering an action, if you *think* it *might* be disloyal, it probably *is* disloyal. If you think it *might* be disloyal and you don't want to tell your partner, it's *definitely* disloyal.

The Duty of Honesty

Of course, this means you do not lie, but it also means you treat your partners with good faith and fair dealing. All shareholders in a closely held corporation owe it to each other to act honestly.[11] The Duty of Honesty is violated when one partner treats another with "unfairly prejudicial conduct." Courts have interpreted the phrase to mean conduct that frustrates shareholders' *reasonable expectations*.[12] Put together, The Duty of Honesty is violated when you violate your partner' reasonable *expectations*.

This begs the question, "What are reasonable expectations?" Reasonable expectations are controlled first by the writings between the parties, usually a *Member (or Shareholder) Control Agreement*, *By-Laws*, and an *Operating Agreement* (which we'll discuss in detail in Chapter 2). These documents set the rules for operating the company. For example, the Control Agreement might permit borrowing money *only* if *all* partners agree, or it might guarantee employment for as long as a partner remains a partner.

---

11   Minn. Stat. § 302A.751, subd. 1(b)(3).

12   *Gunderson v. Alliance of Computer Prof'ls, Inc., 628 N.W.2d 173, 186* (Minn. Ct. App. 2001), review granted (Minn. July 24, 2001), and appeal dismissed (Minn. Aug. 17, 2001).

It's critical that you create these agreements at the *inception* of the partnership, when everyone is thinking about how great business will be. Creating these documents, with the help of your Bulldog, will reveal any fundamental disagreements. Once relationships break down, everyone will have different memories of how the business was intended to operate. If Evans had an agreement guaranteeing lifelong employment, Blesi could not have fired him.

In the absence of a specific agreement, *reasonable expectations* are determined by examining the understanding that objectively reasonable shareholders would have reached if they had settled the issue at the beginning. This creates a situation ripe for litigation.

The Blesi-Evans case gives us a good example. Evans and Blesi did *not* have an agreement as to lifetime employment. Under current law, when Blesi fired Evans, the court would have had to determine whether the two partners, 25 years earlier, had each *expected* lifetime employment. Factors to be considered in determining whether a shareholder's expectation of continued employment are reasonable include whether (1) the shareholder made a capital investment in the company; (2) continued employment could be considered part of the shareholder's investment; (3) the shareholder's salary could be considered a de facto dividend; and (4) continued employment was a significant reason for making the investment.[13]

In reality, however, a minority shareholder who is dismissed from employment generally finds himself without a remedy,

---

13 Ibid.

unless he is protected by an employment contract or a share-holder's agreement.[14] Blesi would argue that Evans was not protected, because he didn't make a capital investment (Blesi *lent* him the money). Continued employment was neither part of the investment, nor a significant reason for making it (it was never discussed). Further, Evans' salary was not related to profits, and therefore not a de facto dividend. On the other hand, Evans would argue that his loan, when repaid, *was* a capital investment, and part of the original deal was that he would get a job and own half the company, so lifetime employment *was* assumed. Lawyers could fight over this issue for a long time.

This is just one example of how the lack of strong early documentation can lead to big legal fees when the fighting begins. When partners have strong early agreements, their expectations are written down. No amount of piety nor wit nor all their tears can wash out a word of it.[15] Each partner must live with their written agreements. Corollary to this rule is that if the original agreements are strong and thorough, any *omitted* agreements are unlikely to be enforced. "I assumed lifetime employment," loses force when the agreements address other issues in detail, but do not include that particular guarantee.

---

14   F.H. O'Neal & R. Thompson, O'Neal's Oppression of Minority Shareholders § 3:06, at 38 (3d ed. 1985) (footnotes omitted). *See also Jenkins v. Haworth, Inc.*, 572 F. Supp. 591 (W.D. Mich. 1983); *Keating v. BBDO Int'l, Inc.*, 438 F. Supp. 676 (S.D.N.Y. 1977).

15   "*The Moving Finger* writes; and, having writ, Moves on: nor all thy Piety nor Wit Shall lure it back to cancel half a Line, Nor all thy Tears wash out a Word of it." - Omar Khayyám.

The *Duty of Honesty* means all partners are entitled to satisfaction of their reasonable expectations. When the initial agreements are clear and strong, everybody's expectations are clear, and all partners know what they are. These expectations define the Duty of Honesty beyond just "not lying." Strong agreements may not force a bad business partner to be honest and candid, but at least everyone will be using the same rule book.

The Duty of Openness

Openness, or full disclosure, is an *extension* of honesty. Openness means not only telling the truth, but telling the *whole* truth. Candor between partners is critical. It allows them to make informed decisions, and builds trust. Full disclosure is also the law. Partners owe each other a fiduciary duty to disclose to each other *all* material information *fully* and *fairly*.[16]

For example, a clear violation of the Duty of Openness would arise if one partner recommended a certain vendor, but did *not* reveal that the vendor was paying a handsome commission. A partner might also violate this duty by concealing that he had been diagnosed with a health issue affecting his ability to do his job. The Duty of Openness always arises when a partner is considering a potential corporate opportunity, or engaging in self-dealing.

The *easy* rule is to tell the truth, the *whole* truth, and nothing but the truth. This means disclosing *all* material facts of which the

---

16 *TSC Industries, Inc. v. Northway, Inc.*, 426 U.S. 438, 449, 96 S.Ct. 2126, 2132, 48 L.Ed.2d 757 (1976); *Rosenblatt v. Getty Oil Co.*, Del.Supr. 493 A.2d 929, 944 (1985).

partner is aware, which could adversely or significantly affect a particular transaction. This would certainly include any financial interest the partner has in a particular transaction.

The Duty of Openness requires full disclosure to your partners. This is not a complicated principle. "Full" means "full," not "Full except for..." You must disclose *all* material facts. If you find yourself creating exceptions based on what is "material," you're probably making excuses. If you even think something might be of interest to your partners, you should disclose it.

The Rest of the Story

The next meeting between Blesi and Evans derailed the partnership for good. According to court testimony, Blesi shouted at Evans, slammed the door, accused him of incompetence and dishonesty, and threatened to fire Evans' son from the sales force if Evans did not resign voluntarily. Evans signed the resignation and the informal minutes that the Blesi's attorney had prepared.

But three days later, after consulting with his Bulldog, Evans changed his mind. He sent a notice of revocation of his signatures on the Resignation and the Informal Action of Shareholders. Blesi's attorney advised him to ignore it. Blesi followed this advice and ignored Evans.

Evans was not paid his salary, was refused his annual bonus, and Blesi refused to make the yearly contribution for Evans to the company's pension and profit-sharing trusts. Approximately one month in advance of the stock transfer meeting with Evans, Blesi had had documents prepared empowering him to disqualify employees from eligibility for pension and profit-sharing payments

13

if employment was terminated before the end of the fiscal year. On the last day of the company's fiscal year in 1982, after Evans' earlier resignation, Blesi then invoked this disqualification clause and refused to make the payments.

Of course, the parties ended up in court. Blesi was found to have violated his fiduciary duty. The jury awarded Evans damages and reinstatement, but the judge set aside Evans' reinstatement because "the extreme acrimony" between the former friends would adversely affect corporate operations.

Unfortunately, this type of tragic end to a 30-year friendship is a common one. However, it is avoidable. Evans and Blesi both made mistakes along the way and missed opportunities to salvage their relationship. These mistakes began in their very first set of agreements.

The Bulldog is loyal, eager to please, and gentle unless provoked. Before entering a partnership, commit to the fundamental principles of loyalty, honesty and openness. And bark loudly if you suspect your partner is violating this duty.

Chapter 2:

Good Founding Documents Make Good Partners

D on Thomas sat slumped in the chair of the deposition room.

"I went to pick up my daughter at high school. When she wasn't at the front door, I looked around and spotted her at the far end of the parking lot, talking to a boy. 'Cute,' I thought, until I got closer. My 15-year-old daughter is talking to a 19-year-old boy. This guy is two years out of high school! He's wearing jeans with no shirt, sitting on the tailgate of his F150, drinking from a brown paper sack."

This was the inauspicious start for Jack, the guy with the bottle, and Tonya, the 15-year-old. They were romantic partners in a rocky, off-and-on relationship for 25 years. They had three children together but were never married.

Over the years, Jack built a successful business. He had no college education, but he was smart and he worked hard. He understood people and he understood the needs of oil companies in North Dakota. Oil companies need material to build roads. Oilfield roads need a volcanic rock called *scoria*, the lightweight, easily crushable and absorbent orange rock found on Little League infields.

Jack bought land, dug up the scoria, and sold it to oil companies during the Bakken oil boom. He bought more land and sold more scoria. He made millions by buying ranch land and selling the scoria beneath it.

The land was always owned by Jack. The oil company contracts were always with Jack. Tonya helped out with the business from time to time, but was never employed by the company, and never owned any part of it. When they were together, Jack gave Tonya money as she needed it, but she was never on the payroll. When they split up, she claimed to have been his business partner, and sued for half of his $20 million business. I was Jack's lawyer. My job was to find a resolution that would bring Jack peace of mind, and still preserve his net worth.

Tonya's lawyer had a difficult job. She claimed to own half the business, but had no documents to support her position. Her lawyer had to prove Tonya was a partner in a business where no partnership had been formed. He was trying to prove a *de facto* partnership.[17]

A *de facto* partnership is created when two or more people have combined their property, labor, and skill in an enterprise as *co-owners* for the purpose of *joint* profit.[18] The *substance*,

---

17 Of note, North Dakota does not recognize common law marriage. Tonya's lawyer did not have the option of suing for a marital divorce.

18 *Cyrus v. Cyrus*, 242 Minn. 180, 183-84, 64 N.W.2d 538, 541 (1954).

rather than the name of the arrangement, determines the legal relationship.[19] In 1933, the Supreme Court recognized that when a business is operated without a formal structure, the business is treated as a partnership.[20] In the case of *Manufacturers Bldg., Inc. v. Heller*,[21] the court ruled, in short, that when two or more parties create a business together and do not formalize the business entity, it will be automatically deemed to be a partnership.

By the time the lawyer gets the case, the feuding partners usually have lost trust in each other. Honest people have differing memories, while dishonest people will make things up. Any later dispute about what the partners *expected* and *agreed* to comes down to the *documents* they signed when the business started. So, the Bulldog insists on creating strong documents at the outset.

The fastest horse doesn't always win the race, but that's the way to bet. In close corporations, written agreements do not always *prove* shareholder expectations, but they are the best evidence, and courts will rely on them in a dispute.[22]

Tonya claimed that Jack had promised her half the business. She said he called it, "Our business," but she had nothing in writing.

---

19 *Randall Co. v. Briggs*, 189 Minn. 175, 178, 248 N.W. 752, 754 (1933).

20 *Halvorson v. Geurkink*, 238 Minn. 371, 376, 56 N.W.2d 793, 796 (1953); *Johnson v. Corser*, 34 Minn. 355, 359-60, 25 N.W. 799, 801 (1885).

21 *Manufacturers Bldg., Inc. v. Heller*, 306 Minn. 180, 182, 235 N.W.2d 825, 826-27 (1975).

22 *Gunderson v. Alliance of Computer Prof'ls, Inc.*, 628 N.W.2d 173, 186 (Minn. Ct. App. 2001), review granted (Minn. July 24, 2001), and appeal dismissed (Minn. Aug. 17, 2001).

She never invested capital. She was never even on the payroll. She couldn't remember exactly when these promises were made. She could not produce witnesses who heard the promises. There were no documents to prove her case. The lawsuit dragged out over three years.

Strong formation documents are critical. Some of these are boilerplate, but three of them are substantial agreements that affect the operation of the partnership.

The first of these is a *Control Agreement* governing the partners' relationship. The second is a set of *Bylaws* governing the company operation. The third is a *Buy-Sell Agreement*, governing what happens when a partner departs.

The purpose of these documents at the beginning is to maximize the chance of a smooth resolution at the end. In the beginning, neither partner knows if they will be the one who gets sick, or dies, or wants to retire. So the partners are thinking more in terms of what would be *fair* to both at some future date, rather than in trying to turn the rules to their own advantage. Your Bulldog can provide balanced agreements covering a variety of unseen scenarios.

Control Agreements

Member Control Agreements (for an LLC) and Shareholder Control Agreements (for a corporation) are contracts between the owners of the business. These contracts contain the agreements of the business owners regarding many matters, most of which will never come up. But when these issues do arise, the documents govern how the issues will be handled.

Control Agreements set the rules for potential problems that the new partners don't think of, and expect never to come up. Events that "will never happen to us" actually happen all the time. In a Control Agreement, partners spell out how they will handle future changes. Your Bulldog can point out scenarios that you otherwise might not anticipate.

Make no mistake, change will come. What happens if one of the partners files for bankruptcy? Do his creditors get the stock, and the control that goes with it? A good Control Agreement avoids this problem by giving the company a first option to purchase the bankrupt partner's shares. The creditors can still make claims for the *value* of the shares, but they cannot interfere with operations.

What if a partner dies, or gets divorced? Does the company have to take on his widow or ex-wife as a partner? Without a Control Agreement, these outsiders will have claims on the partner's ownership interest, including voting rights. The Control Agreement solves this problem the same way, by giving the company the first right to buy the partner's shares. The widower or ex-spouse receives value for the ownership, but the remaining owners are not forced to take them on as partners.

What if a partner wants to sell her shares to a third party, and the remaining partners do not want to be in business with the buyer? The Control Agreement solves this issue by requiring any partner to provide any remaining owners a *right of first refusal* to buy the interest on the same terms as the third-party buyer.

What if a partner can't work because of disability, criminal conviction, or retirement? Each of these situations creates different

19

expectations. A good Control Agreement will dictate what happens in each.

What if one partner wants to borrow money and another partner doesn't? What if the partners are in a deadlock? The Control Agreement will set forth the required votes to approve important decisions outside the normal course of business.

The Control Agreement will also set forth the rights of minority shareholders; the owners' right to be indemnified if sued, and any other potential problems owners agree on. Lifetime employment expectations, if any, will be outlined in the Control Agreement.

Over the course of decades of operation, almost all companies will experience one or more of these events. Without a good Control Agreement, such an event can be disastrous. A good Control Agreement sets out the rules for everybody and will save the company stress, operational disruption and legal fees.

One critical piece of many Control Agreements is the Buy-Sell Agreement. The Buy-Sell agreement sets forth the process for valuation of the departing partner's ownership. Some lawyers put the Buy-Sell Agreement within the Control Agreement, but your Bulldog will prefer to keep it as a separate document, on its own.

Buy-Sell Agreements

When a partner leaves a closely held company, two things are usually true: the value of the departing partner's ownership is unclear, and the remaining partners do not want to be in business with an outside party who might have a claim on the ownership interest, whether it's a creditor, ex-spouse, heir, or outside investor. A Buy-Sell Agreement solves these problems by setting out the valuation process, and stating the respective rights of the company and the partners when one owner departs.

There are many reasons a partner might leave a closely-held company, but almost all fall into two broad categories. A partner may leave (or be forced from) the company when no longer available to work because of death, disability or misconduct. Sometimes an owner desires (or is required) to transfer his ownership to a third party, for example, in a procedure for the benefit of creditors, or in bankruptcy, divorce or a voluntary sale to a third party. The Buy-Sell Agreement protects the company and other partners in these situations.

When a partner dies, the surviving partners can be squeezed between their desire to help their partner's family, and their need to conduct business unimpeded by estate issues, and without the influence of heirs. A Buy-Sell Agreement should require the estate to offer the company and other partners the option to buy the shares, usually within 60 or 90 days, at a value determined under the agreement. Closely-held companies should carry *Key Man Insurance* to fund the purchase. A Bulldog will likely set the purchase price as the amount of the death benefit of the policy. This gives the company available funds to pay for the ownership, and enables the estate to efficiently liquidate the ownership value. However, this also means that the company must pay the premiums along the way, and to regularly adjust the benefit to roughly equal the value of the ownership. These burdens are slight when compared to the disruption of a partner's death, compounded by dealing with the heirs, or an estate battle.

21

If a partner becomes totally disabled and can't work, it's similar to a partner's death, but not exactly the same. Disability is often the result of a tragic accident or illness. Again, the remaining partners want to help their partner's family, but do not necessarily want her Trustee or Power of Attorney to influence business operations.

The agreement must have a clear definition of what is a disability. Out of work for six months? Maybe forever? Does it extend to include addiction or depression? What about paralysis or blindness, which do not necessarily make it impossible to work? This is an example of the need to create these definitions at the beginning, when the partners do not yet know who might be the disabled one.

If a partner meets the definition of disability, the Buy-Sell Agreement should provide an option to purchase the partner's interest, at the price set by a process defined in the agreement (more on valuation below). Unlike in death, there will be no life insurance policy to fund the buyout. However, in such case, payments can be made over time and still take care of the partner and his family.

A partner can be forced out of the company because of a variety of misconduct. These range from felony convictions to sexual harassment to violations of company policies. Misconduct clauses can be punitive. Some Buy-Sell Agreements mandate forfeiture of ownership for serious offenses against the company. This harsh remedy might not be legally enforceable, but any reasonably calculated purchase price is generally valid. Most Buy-Sell Agreements have a separate provision for pricing the ownership if the departing partner is guilty of misconduct. It's no surprise that victimized partners are less inclined to make sure their former partner is taken care of.

Insolvency and divorce are similar in the context of departing partners. The remaining partners don't want the business disrupted by outside parties like creditors or vicious divorce attorneys. Without a Buy-Sell Agreement, outsiders can attach the partner's actual business ownership interest. Ownership carries more rights than just its financial value. Partners can have voting rights, the right to select board members, and the right to veto major decisions, among others. The divorce/insolvency provision will give the company and partners an option to buy the ownership interest ahead of the creditors. The company buys the ownership interest, converting the departing partner's ownership asset to cash. Thus, the ownership interest is out of reach of the outsiders (it also means the insolvent partner is no longer a partner, which has consequences discussed later). The outsiders can chase the cash, but this will minimize the impact on the business operation.

Sometimes, a partner just wants to sell his ownership to a third party. This is like a husband leaving a marriage, but replacing himself with a man his wife has never met. Again, the remaining partners may not want to be forced to partner with the outsider, so the Buy-Sell Agreement will have a specific restriction against transferring ownership without company approval. There should also be a provision for the company to buy the ownership on the same terms. These provisions can lead to a sequence of events and entanglements that read like a mystery novel.

The departing partner tells her partners she's leaving. The remaining partners are negotiating with their departing partner on one hand, and sizing up their potential new partner on the other. Do they want this partner? Does she bring value or disruption? Do they just want to buy the ownership? Would they be overpaying? Meanwhile, the suitor and the company are simultaneously conducting due diligence on each other.

Unlike other scenarios, the value of the buyout is not set by the Buy-Sell Agreement. It's set by the terms of the *bona fide* offer, so the price is fluid. And the remaining partners may have conflicting motives, depending on what they decide to do. If the company buys back the ownership, they will want the valuation to be low. If the company accepts the new partner, they will want the valuation to be as high as possible, which increases the value of their own ownership. They may want the new partner to bring additional capital, in which case they would want her to pay as little as possible for the ownership, and have more to invest as capital. Unless they want her to invest less capital.... The nuances go on and on.

Valuation is at the heart of any partner buyout. The valuation provision of the Buy-Sell Agreement will explain how the purchase price of the ownership interest will be determined under whatever provision the partner is departing. There are many processes that work well.

Some documents use a version of the, "I cut, you choose" method to set the price. In this resolution strategy, two parties want to evenly divide the last piece of cake. One of them cuts the cake and the other gets to choose her piece. In the business divorce context, this means that one party presents an offer to the other, and agrees that he will either buy or sell at that price.

This seemingly simple solution is fraught with peril. It really only works with fungible commodities, not with partnerships. Partners are never on exactly the same footing. A partner who has more capital can make a low offer that he knows the other partner can't afford to pay. If one partner really wants to retire, he's at a disadvantage. And this system really goes off the rails when dealing with death or third-party creditors, where the parties are on completely separate footing.

The Bulldog will prefer a more regimented version of this principle. When a shareholder departs, the company pays for a *neutral* appraiser to value the ownership interest. If either the buyer or seller disagrees with the appraisal, then she can pay for another valuation. If the second is within 20% of the first (either way), the first valuation sets the price. If the second is outside this range, then the other party can choose to either accept the average of the first and second, or conduct a third appraisal at their own expense. Then the price is set by the *middle* valuation of the three. This process actually creates a series of "I cut, you choose" transactions. At each stage, the parties are motivated to reach agreement, because there will be no change unless the amount determined is truly reasonable.

It's inevitable that at some point, a partner will be separated from the company. It's critical to have a good Buy-Sell Agreement in place before this happens. Without one, the departure of a partner can seriously disrupt the business. An outsider who becomes an owner cannot be forced to sell. If the remaining partners don't want him, they're motivated to buy him out. This gives the outsider leverage to negotiate a high price for his interest. The remaining partners may be left with a Hobson's choice between the long-term problems of financing a high buyout payment, or keeping an unwanted outsider as a partner. A good Buy-Sell Agreement avoids this problem.

Operating Agreements and Bylaws

The operating rules of a closely-held company are found in either an Operating Agreement (for an LLC) or its Bylaws (for a corporation). For our purpose, we can refer to them both as the Bylaws. Bylaws contain rules, regulations and provisions for how the company makes fundamental decisions. Its purpose is to dictate how the owners will make the business's internal operating decisions. The bylaws are another writing that states the owners' reasonable expectations.

When a dispute arises, a strong set of bylaws can lead to an efficient resolution of a reasonable disagreement. For example, how many board members, and how are they selected? How many votes are needed to borrow $10,000? What about a million?

Good bylaws enable the company to create its own operating rules. In most states, a company with no bylaws will be controlled by a statutory set of rules. These rules are general rules and may not be the right ones for a particular business. Bylaws can be very flexible, so long as all partners agree on them. It is better to create the operating rules you want than to be stuck with the state's general rules.

The Rest of the Story

In the case of Tonya and Jack, Tonya's case didn't have legs. If she had really wanted to be a part of the business, she should have insisted on getting the right documents in place at the very beginning. Without written agreements, she couldn't prove her claim. If Tonya really thought that she owned half of Jack's business, she should have documented it. Had she asked in the beginning, Jack may or may not have agreed to have her as a partner. But later, when the trouble started, Tonya had no formal documents, so she had no leverage. She finally gave up after three years of litigation and stress that could have been avoided. She finally settled for a place to live, some money set aside for the kids, and a few minor concessions.

Jack and Tonya's case is extreme, but the absence of strong, written agreements leads to litigation in less dramatic circumstances. Issues not addressed in the original documents can become problems later, when partners' interests diverge. If one partner dies suddenly, do I have to take on his wife as a partner? If not, how do we price the purchase of her shares? What if one of us becomes disabled or incarcerated? Strong original documents contain the answers to these questions and many more.

Chapter 3:

Set Reasonable Expectations with Good Planning

Twin Bridges was a family-owned limited partnership, which owned a 250-acre parcel of real estate outside Philadelphia. The partners of Twin Bridges were the seven surviving children of Katharine Draper, plus their children and spouses. Mrs. Draper established the partnership in 1985 for estate planning purposes, and named two of her children, her daughter Katherine Draper Schutt, and son, Ford B. Draper, Jr., as general partners with authority to make all major decisions. The other siblings were all limited partners with no management authority.

After their mother's death, Katherine Schutt and Ford Draper disagreed on some important issues, thereby effectively creating gridlock within the partnership. To circumvent this problem, Schutt and most of the limited partners, who collectively held 87% of the interests and voting power in Twin Bridges, decided to pursue a solution without involving Draper and his two sons. On August 16, 2006, the partners aligned with Schutt acted by written consent to amend the Partnership Agreement, and then to merge the partnership into a newly-formed limited partnership with a different governance structure. The new partnership agreement provided for a third general partner, their sister Prudence Draper Osborn. These actions did not change any partner's economic interests in the partnership, but did change the governance structure. Draper lost "negative control," meaning he moved from 50% control so he could no longer block actions by Schutt and Osborn.

The same day they took control, Katherine Schutt and Prudence Osborn, in favor of the limited partners aligned with them ("Schutt Group") filed a lawsuit seeking court approval of their amendment to the Partnership Agreement, which fundamentally gave the Schutt Group control of the business. The whole thing ended up in court. A closer examination of what happened demonstrates how Mrs. Draper's original failure to plan led to family division and an acrimonious battle.

Mrs. Draper owned Beverly Farms, a 250-acre estate in Chards Ford, Pennsylvania.[23] Mrs. Draper's house and the surrounding area were the only developed portions of the Property. Two areas of Beverly Farms located near Mrs. Draper's house, known as the "Play Yard" and "Shop" sites, were viable for development.

In December 1985, Ford Draper, Jr. suggested to his mother that creating a limited partnership to hold Beverly Farms for future development could provide immediate tax benefits to her, and future benefits for her children and grandchildren. With the help of her lawyers, Ford Draper assisted Mrs. Draper in forming

23 *Twin Bridges Ltd. Partnership v. Draper*, 2007 WL 2744609 (Del, Ch. Sept. 14, 2007).

the Twin Bridges Limited Partnership to enable Mrs. Draper to remove Beverly Farms from her estate and establish a governance structure (the "Original Partnership Agreement" or "OPA") that would govern collaboration on any future development or sale of the property. Mrs. Draper contributed the title to Beverly Farms as the initial capital of Twin Bridges. She then gifted about 30% of the partnership interest in equal amounts to her seven children and retained the remaining interest. Over the remainder of her lifetime, Mrs. Draper gifted the interest she had retained in Twin Bridges to her children, their spouses, and her grandchildren. She did not provide any plans or instructions regarding the development of the Property.

At its inception, Twin Bridges had two general partners, Draper and Schutt. The OPA also named Mrs. Draper and five of her children, Osborn, Ellen Draper Mahalingham (now Ellen Chadwick), Elizabeth Avery Draper, Reeve Draper Dinneen (now Reeve Draper), and James Avery Draper, IV, as limited partners. Collectively, the two general partners and six limited partners owned all of the original Twin Bridges partnership. Over time, the spouses and children of the original general and limited partners were admitted as additional or substitute limited partners. As of August 16, 2006, five family blocs each held approximately 17 percent of the outstanding interests in Twin Bridges, and Draper and his family held approximately 13 percent.

Under the OPA, Mrs. Draper named Ford Draper, Jr. as the initial managing partner of Twin Bridges, and gave him authority to conduct the ordinary and usual activities and business of the Partnership. This general authority begs the question: what *is* the "ordinary and usual" activity of a partnership that holds land which

31

has not been developed, but could be? Although the OPA named Draper as Managing Partner, it required both Draper and Schutt, as general partners, to consent "to all major decisions affecting the Partnership business." Contrary to Draper's sole authority to conduct "ordinary and usual" activity, the OPA also gave the two general partners "equal voice in all decisions with respect to the overall management, control, and policies of the Partnership." Thus, for at least all major decisions affecting Twin Bridges' business, Draper and Schutt had to *agree* on a course of action. In addition, the OPA expressly prohibits *limited* partners from participating "in the management of the Partnership business." The OPA could be amended by a majority of the limited partners, but not so as to allow the limited partners to take part in the control of the business, unless *all* partners, general *and* limited, consented to such an amendment. Thus, Draper had control of the business with only 13% ownership. He had full authority over "ordinary and usual" activity, and a veto over any "major decision" or change of partnership control. In a family situation, where all owners would expect to be treated equally, this imbalance was a recipe for disaster. Mrs. Draper did not anticipate this problem, and failed to plan for it.

Before Mrs. Draper's death, the Partnership's decisions largely related to the maintenance of the Property. Although Draper and Schutt disagreed over the future development of Beverly Farms, Twin Bridges operated relatively smoothly. However, after Mrs. Draper died, the partners of Twin Bridges soon began to discuss potential options for developing the land. These discussions reflected disagreements among the partners, and over time, grew more discordant as partners advanced divergent ideas. Disagreements arose, for example, over who might purchase the main house, and where new development, if any, could be started.

Within months of Mrs. Draper's death in 2005, the family met to discuss overall objectives and planning relating to development of the property. Although the family disagreed on how the property should be divided, they agreed to investigate the creation of a detailed land plan. Draper then collaborated with Brandywine Conservancy, Inc. to determine how the land might be divided equitably among those partners interested in building on it. In December 2005, the family met a second time to discuss development of the Play Yard site. According to Draper, Schutt didn't want anyone to build there because it would obstruct the view from the main house, in which she was interested. In March 2006, Schutt reiterated her desire to avoid development of the Play Yard site.

In April 2006, Brandywine Conservancy presented its development plan to Twin Bridges. Over the next month, the family debated how the Property should be divided. Both Schutt and Draper expressed interest in purchasing the main house. In addition, they disagreed on how the surrounding property should be developed and made available for division among the remaining partners. Mrs. Draper had not planned for this discord, and the OPA did not contain a methodology for deciding who gets what in case of dispute.

The general partners continued to disagree. However, due to the structure of the OPA, no resolution could be reached unless both Draper and Schutt unanimously consented to the development plan. Schutt and the vast majority of the limited partners then determined that a new partnership structure was needed to break the deadlock. In July 2006, the Schutt Group (excluding Draper's family) began discussing how they could more effectively manage the Property. After considering alternatives, the Schutt Group determined that a management structure with three general partners would reduce the likelihood of deadlock and facilitate decision making. But because the dispute was already ongoing, it was too late for this solution. Draper would not consent to such amendment, and he had a veto.

So, the Schutt Group resolved to merge Twin Bridges into a new limited partnership with a new partnership agreement providing for *three* general partners, and dissolve the original Twin Bridges Partnership. The OPA, however, did not include a merger provision (another planning failure). Therefore, Schutt and the limited partners (other than Draper and his family) first amended the OPA to include, among other things, a merger provision (the "Amendment"). The new provision enabled partners holding two-thirds of the interest in Twin Bridges to approve a merger, and explicitly authorized a merger into another limited partnership. That would have the effect of amending the OPA. They also created TB II, L.P. ("TB II"), a new partnership that provided for management by three general partners. Schutt and the limited partners planned to vote to approve the Amendment, then merge Twin Bridges into TB II at the next family meeting, scheduled for August 16, 2006.

At the August 16 family meeting, Schutt announced to Draper and his family that she and the limited partners aligned with her had decided to take this action. Draper and his sons had no prior notice of Schutt's intentions. Schutt Group essentially presented the plan as a *fait accompli*. Because Schutt and the allied limited partners collectively owned more than the necessary two-thirds interest needed to amend the OPA, they executed written consents, amending the OPA to add a merger provision.

The Amendment purported to effect four changes relevant to the dispute:

(1) it explicitly recognized the Partnership's ability to merge with or into another limited partnership or other business entity;

(2) it authorized the approval of a merger by partners having, in the aggregate, two-thirds of the interest in the capital of the Partnership;

(3) it authorized either general partner, acting alone, to execute a merger agreement on behalf of the Partnership; and

(4) pursuant to Section 17-211(g) of DRULPA, it authorized an agreement of merger that would affect an amendment of the OPA. The Amendment ignored Draper's veto over "major decisions".

Within an hour of enacting the Amendment, the Schutt Group voted by written consent under the pertinent provisions of the OPA, as amended, to merge Twin Bridges into TB II (the "Merger"). Based upon the Schutt Group's consents, the Amendment and the Merger became effective in that order as of August 16, 2006. Once Twin Bridges merged into TB II, the OPA ceased to control, and the new partnership agreement of TB II (the "New Partnership Agreement" or "NPA"), attached as Schedule I to the

Agreement and Plan of Merger ("Merger Agreement"), became controlling. Thus Osborn became the third general partner and became involved in management. Draper's veto over this action was bypassed because this was a new partnership, not an amendment to the OPA. The *coup d'état* was complete.

On August 16, 2006, the same day Schutt Group took control, they also commenced a lawsuit seeking court approval of their actions. Draper counter-sued for breach of fiduciary duty, among other things.

Agree Early on the Purpose of the Business

The Twin Bridges story beautifully illustrates why partners should agree on why they're in business from the very beginning. Was the purpose of Twin Bridges to preserve the family land in the historic Twin Bridges district? Or was the purpose to maximize financial return on real estate sitting in the direct path of Philadelphia's expansion? Mrs. Draper, or the OPA, could have reasonably directed the partnership to foster either of these goals. Without a stated purpose, Draper and Schutt could reasonably have disagreed about the best way to proceed. In fact, they did disagree, and ended up in a bitter dispute. If the purpose had been stated, that statement could have served as the "tiebreaker" in determining the direction of the partnership.

Usually, the choice between purposes is more subtle than in Twin Bridges. For example, when two thirty-year old friends decide to start an accounting firm, they can be doing it for *different* reasons. One might be intent on growing the firm to 100 accountants and eventually merging with a large firm. He's willing to make the firm his life's work. The other partner might want their firm to be a small lifestyle business, where he can work hard, make a good living but still keep his family as the first priority. The first partner will want to get top shelf office space, take on debt, and work 20-hour days. The second partner will not be willing to do these things, as they would adversely impact his family life. Like ketchup and ice cream, both of these purposes are good, but they do not work well together. We'll discuss more about selecting the right partner in Chapter 4.

Problems are inevitable when partners disagree on purpose. Married couples can either have children, or not have children, but they cannot do both. Partners can either take action to grow the company, or not take such action. They cannot do both. Businesses make these choices all the time. Should a manufacturing firm own its factory property or lease it? Shall you go after the big contract or stay with your mid-sized customers? How much should you spend on travel? These questions will be answered by looking at your business purpose.

If Mrs. Draper had declared that she was forming Twin Bridges so the land could be preserved, all partners would have expected that when they came on board. Draper and Schutt could have worked together to serve this purpose. By not stating her purpose, Mrs. Draper left the decision up to a combination of descendants who could be expected to reasonably disagree on the best way to proceed.

Decide Early on How to Resolve Disputes

"Dead" is half of the word "deadlock." This is apt. When a partnership reaches deadlock, it's halfway to its death. Even reasonable and well-intentioned partners can disagree on serious

37

matters, and in some cases, there's no room for compromise. Do we accept the offer we just received to sell the business? Should Twin Bridges develop their family land or preserve it? Should we buy a building to expand? Such issues cannot be solved by meeting halfway. The business must have a process in place to break such deadlocks.

A deadlock is when the management of the company cannot agree on a fundamental aspect of the business, such that the business cannot function properly. Good partners will disagree, but work out their differences. When the partners cannot agree, the business must have a process in place to break such deadlocks. This process should be set forth in the original company agreements.

In Twin Bridges, Mrs. Draper made the common mistake of putting two general partners in charge, but not stating what happens when they cannot agree. She could have named a third partner as a tiebreaker. She could have given the managing partner the decision. She could have dictated that they hire a neutral third party to decide a deadlock. Because she did not put a process in place, it was almost inevitable that the partnership would end up in court.

There are myriad processes that work to break deadlock. The control agreement should require super majority, or even unanimous consent to take particular action, like selling the business, borrowing money, or requiring a capital call. The practical result of such a provision is that such action will not be taken unless almost all the partners agree. This default to the status quo will keep the business moving while the partners debate whether to take major action. Another good method is to set up a tie-breaker system. The agreements can give "in case of a tie" votes to one of the partners or to a third party. The tie-breaker can be given to the President, whoever holds that office. If there are owners who are not decision makers, they can be given the tie-breaking vote. Another method is to set up a quasi-judicial process, whereby the partners present their cases to a neutral third party, and must abide by the decision.

Whatever the process for breaking deadlock, it should be agreed upon at the very start of the business. At that time, the parties have no idea which partner will be advantaged by any system, so they will be most likely to come up with a fair process. The parties will not be able to decide on a process at the time of the dispute, because the advantages that any process might provide will be clearer, and no one will agree to a process they cannot win.

Good Planning Comes from Strong Communications

Strong communication skills are critical to a successful partnership. Regardless of how well-intentioned the partners may be, if they do not communicate well, they will not have a strong partnership. It's notable in the Twin Bridges case, the Schutt Group did not communicate their changes to Draper until they presented it as a *fait accompli*. By excluding Draper from the communications process, they insured the matter would go to court.

Communication Must be Full and Open

To clearly express your thoughts verbally, you must first think clearly. Clear thinking means focusing on the heart of the matter without distraction. Clear communication is the product of full understanding. To reach this level, partners must remove any temptation to parse the truth or withhold information. Keeping secrets from partners is a ticket to the courthouse. A partnership can overcome an occasional heated, but sincere, argument. It cannot survive a loss of trust.

This is a good time to talk about sailboats. In sailing, the bow of the boat must be kept absolutely clean because any little debris interferes with the speed of the boat. If a piece of seaweed gets caught on the front of the boat, it will destroy the perfectly aerodynamic design of the hull. You must get rid of the seaweed.

Likewise, clear communication is achieved by discarding or ignoring all of the ancillary matters and honestly focusing on facts. A fair question arises: How do you get rid of the seaweed?

You communicate clearly by fully understanding the various aspects of any controversial position. This preparation provides the ability to understand the impact your position will have on your partners. For example, if you really believe you're undercompensated, you should make that belief known. But not before you perform a full analysis of the impact of your request on your partners. Do you really produce more for the business, or do you just work longer hours?

Every complicated situation has a solution that is quick, easy and wrong. What is obvious is not always correct. I recently heard a politician (not a trained economist) say that he can rely on his common sense with regard to economic policy. However, economic experts disagreed with him. Government economic policy is not a "common sense" issue. Any act will have far-reaching conse-quences that are invisible to those who do not have the deep understanding of the economy that professionals must master.

Clear communication can solve potentially difficult problems. For example, if one partner is responsible for operations, and the other for generating sales, it may be true that the business will fail if either of them fails. Imagine the road warrior sales partner resents his extensive travel, while the operations partner resents that he never gets to leave town. If the partners discuss these issues, perhaps they can reach a solution whereby the operations partner takes over some of the sales trips. A lawyer friend of mine was great at generating business, but felt guilty that he was enjoying dinner and golf with clients while his partner was stuck "doing all the grunt work." He brought this up to his partner, who shared that he felt guilty about being able to focus on legal work while his partner had to be out schmoozing with clients all the time. Because they discussed the issue, these two discovered that they had the perfect partnership. Each was happy doing work the other did not want to do.

Poor communication can lead to misunderstandings, and then to disaster. A good example of not communicating clearly happened a few years ago when I was driving through upstate New York in a rental car. I was going over the speed limit when I heard the police sirens behind me. I pulled over but I could not find the button to get the window down. I didn't fully understand how to operate the rental car; I had not fully prepared by mapping out all of the buttons before I started driving. As the police officer stood outside of the car, peering through the closed window, demanding that I lower it, I repeatedly pressed the button to make the doors lock and unlock. I was not thinking clearly and the situation grew worse as the stress increased. Finally, I opened the door and stepped out of the car. This definitely raised the intensity of the situation and did not make the policeman happy. With my hands in the air, I explained that I didn't know how to open the windows of the rental car. The police officer understood and was kind enough to let me go with a warning, after I demonstrated that I hadn't been drinking and after he showed me where the window button was located. I was able to avert disaster because I knew that by raising my hands, I would no longer be a potential threat. By quickly communicating why I hadn't opened the window, I relieved the policeman of his fear. It probably helped that I was wearing a nice suit.

Once you fully understand a potentially troubling situation, you can develop the best way to communicate your thoughts to your partner. You will have an idea of how she will react. You can choose whether to say certain things, and how to say them without causing potentially disastrous result.

Imagine, if the road warrior partner trudged grumpily into the operations partner's office and blurted, "I *hate* being on the road. I'm *never* going on the road again!" The already-resentful operations partner reacts angrily with, "I sit here in the office all day while you go to New York and Hollywood and are never here." These two partners are on a slippery slope to breaking up.

On the other hand, if the road warrior thinks everything through first, he can present his position more effectively. He invites his partner to lunch to discuss it. He opens the discussion with, "I'm feeling burned out on the road. I missed my daughter's birthday party again. My wife is mad at me and feeling neglected. Can we figure out a way I can travel less?" The operations partner offers to take some of the trips. Going forward, the partnership is stronger.

If the partners do not plan and communicate well, there's a risk that they will end up in an irresolvable deadlock. The partners each believe they are not getting what they reasonably expected. This will lead to the lawyers' office, the courthouse, and often the end of the partnership.

The Rest of the Story

In the Draper case, after much litigation, the court finally found the amendment valid, and upheld the Schutt Group's control. The Draper family lost their ability to influence the Brandywine development. All the pain (not to mention attorney fees) could have been prevented with proper planning. Mrs. Draper made three mistakes in forming the Twin Bridges partnership. First, she did not define the purpose or long-range plan for the partnership. Second, she gave extraordinary power to a minority owner, Draper. Third, she created a general partnership with two general partners, and no clear plan for removal or succession. Together, these errors led inevitably to deadlock, which could only be resolved by the courts.

Chapter 4:

Choose Your Partners Carefully

I n 2011, good friends Madison and Adams were business partners who formed Minuteman Rentals. Minuteman leased heavy
equipment to oil companies working in the Bakken oilfields.
Starting in 2000, hydraulic fracking stimulated a boom in exploration of the Bakken Formation, and the business prospered.
By July 2014, Minuteman Rentals operated in Williston, North
Dakota and generated more than $10 million in annual revenue,
with no debt. Prospects were bright for the company, as well as
for Madison and Adams.

In December 2013, Hessian Energy approached Adams about
the possibility of acquiring Minuteman Rentals. Over the next
six months, Hessian conducted its due diligence, examining the
company in detail, and meeting many times with Adams and/or
Madison. Adams and Madison were not as careful in their own
investigation of Hessian.

In July 2014, the parties signed agreements transferring 75% of
the shares of Minuteman Rentals to Hessian, with Adams and

Madison each keeping 12.5%. During negotiations, Hessian's principals promised: (a) Hessian would operate Minuteman Rentals properly and run the company well; (b) Hessian would provide a high level of capitalization to Minuteman Rentals, including the purchase of new equipment, to ensure the continued sustained success of Minuteman Rentals; and (c) Hessian would provide Adams and Madison complete financial transparency, including complete access to Minuteman Rentals' books and records, monthly meetings to review the operation, and regular discussion of Minuteman Rentals' finances. As it turned out, Hessian had no intention of keeping these promises.

The problems began immediately after closing, when Madison discovered the undisclosed manner in which Hessian Energy raised funds to pay Madison and Adams for their shares. To pay Madison and Adams, Hessian had taken out a loan of $1 million ("Loan One") from Yorktown Finance, secured by much of Minuteman Rentals' equipment, which had previously been owned outright.

At the direction of Hessian, Minuteman Rentals then loaned Hessian Energy $2.75 million, comprised of the Loan One funds, with the balance satisfied by Minuteman Rentals' own cash on hand, to pay for the acquisition. Hessian paid Madison and Adams for the purchase of Minuteman with their own money!

In November 2014, Minuteman Rentals secured another loan from Yorktown, this time in the amount of $50,000, which was secured by all of Minuteman Rentals' equipment ("Loan 2"), and directed the funds to Hessian. They never repaid the loans.

With the benefit of hindsight, Hessian's intent was clear: Hessian ventured into North Dakota at the height of the oil boom, identified a well-run and fully-capitalized business to buy. Then they purchased it, stripped its assets, and left Madison and Adams holding the bag. For example, immediately following the Closing in July 2014, Madison gave Hessian approximately $500,000.00 of checks made payable to Minuteman Rentals' vendors. The checks had been signed by Madison immediately prior to the execution of the Share Purchase Agreements, were signed on behalf of Minuteman Rentals, and were intended to pay the company's creditors. Hessian never sent the checks to the vendors and actively concealed this fact from Madison and Adams. The vendors went unpaid.

To the same end, Hessian converted the equipment of Minuteman Rentals to other companies owned by Hessian. In April 2016, Minuteman Rentals defaulted on both Loan One and Loan Two, and pledged all of its equipment to Yorktown Finance. Some of this equipment pre-dated Hessian Energy's acquisition of Minuteman Rentals, but was nonetheless sold to Hessian's other subsidiaries at discount prices. Hessian then used these funds to pay down the Yorktown loans without providing Adams and Madison with their twenty-five percent share of the proceeds.

In the midst of these intra-company transfers, the deliberate refusal to pay creditors, and without any notice to Madison and Adams, Minuteman, at Hessian's direction, paid $45,000.00 per month in fictional "management fees" to another affiliated company. Madison and Adams did not receive their share of Minuteman Rentals' distributions.

These troubling facts were not isolated. Hessian failed to keep its promise to adequately capitalize Minuteman Rentals, failed to provide access to Minuteman Rentals' books and records, and failed to honor other contractual obligations to Madison and Adams.

Following closing, Madison and Adams remained salaried employees of Minuteman Rentals, as required by the Share Purchase Agreements. When Madison insisted on receiving access to the company's financial records to determine how the company's funds were being used, he was fired. Adams was similarly fired six months later. At the time of their respective terminations, Minuteman Rentals owed Madison and Adams several hundred thousand dollars in unpaid expense reimbursements.

Madison and Adams came to see me to pursue their rights against Hessian. They felt that they had "done everything right," but as a Bulldog Lawyer, I could see they had made a mess of things. Madison and Adams made one major mistake. They picked the wrong partner.

Pick Partners You Trust

Trust in your business partner is critical. This means you must trust them not only to be honest and to keep your secrets, but also that you must trust them to be good at the work of your business. If you have any doubts about your potential partner's ability to keep any of these three obligations, do not go into business with them.

There's no shortcut to earning trust. Real trust is established by years of knowing each other, in both good and bad times, and by going through shared experience. This is why so often business partners are close friends before they go into business together.

Sometimes two people can start a business without knowing each other well and still succeed, but it's the exception. Success is more likely when the partners trust each other, both personally and professionally, warts and all. In a strong partnership, partners can share ideas, bad news and potential problems without hesitation. To do this, each partner must trust that the others will understand, even in disagreement, that the information is shared for the common good. If a partner tries to cover up a mistake, or blames others for company problems, the partnership will suffer. If one partner is making bad decisions, the others must be able to call it out and know that it will be taken in the spirit offered, to make the business better. This kind of trust is intimate, and is not easily achieved. True trust only comes after knowing someone for years.

I believe the old adage that tough times do not build character, they *reveal* it. It's easy to get along when things are going well, and the biggest disputes are around dividing up profits at year-end. True character is revealed when things get harder. Is your partner courageous or cowardly? Does he try to blame others, or cover up his own mistakes? Does she act with integrity, regardless of who's at fault for a downturn? Does he fight for the business, or fight for himself? If at all possible, it's good to find a partner who you have been through tough times with so you can predict how they will react. With this knowledge, you'll know what to expect when times get tough.

Pick Partners with Complementary Skills

I am not a bean counter. I once had a law partner who watched every penny. This was irritating at times, but at the end of the year, I was always glad *he* was in charge of the money.

You may be strong in operations, but weak at sales. The company needs both. Look for a partner who has the skill set that you do not have. Someone needs to sell, and someone needs to make sure the sales are delivered on time.

People tend to attract people like themselves. Likewise, sellers tend to have similar personalities. But if you and your partner are both focused on selling, who will make the products? Who will monitor the supply chain? On the other hand, if everyone is good at operations, but no one is selling, revenue will dry up fast. Every business needs skills in marketing, sales, operations, management, design and finance. Two people might be able to cover these responsibilities, but at least one partner must be skilled in each of them. If not, you'll have to hire someone who has the missing skills. As the owners, this additional payroll comes right out of your pocket.

Pick a Partner with the Same Business Attitude

Contrary to needing different, complementary skills, partners should have the *same attitude* towards business. According to John Warrilow, in the classic book, *Drilling for Gold*[24], small

24 Warrilow, John, *Drilling for Gold - How Corporations Can Successfully Market To Small Business Owners*, John Wiley & Sons, New York, N.Y. 2002.

business owners can be divided into three general types. Warrillow called these three categories: Mountain Climbers, Freedom Fighters, and Craftspeople.

Mountain Climbers

These people are defined by their need to grow and challenge themselves. They're never satisfied with where they are currently and are always striving to be better. They are compelled to compete and win. Employees often do not like their Mountain Climber boss, but they do respect her. They will be motivated to perform by fear and to seek approval of the boss. Mountain Climbers view money as the scorecard.

Freedom Fighters

These people are motivated by *independence*. They want control of their own time and their own life. Freedom Fighters surround themselves with employees who they like spending time with. Employees often love their Freedom Fighter boss, and are motivated to perform by wanting to please. Freedom Fighters view money as a way to attain freedom.

Craftspeople

These entrepreneurs are driven by the need to *be the best* at what they do. They seek to master their craft. Their business is an extension of themselves. Craftspeople are risk averse, and will have few, if any employees, because nobody is as good at what they do. They view money as a means to keep doing what they enjoy, and often think of their money and the company's money as one pot.

These three types can be illustrated by a new version of an old business fable. A Mountain Climber and a Freedom Fighter were vacationing on a small island. One day, they hired a fishing guide to take them out for a day on the water. The guide was a Craftsperson. As he watched his line in the water, the Mountain Climber had an idea. "You have a good business here," he said to the fisherman. "I would like to invest in two more boats for you."

"Why would I want two more boats?" Asked the Craftsperson.

"Well, the way I figure it, if you had two more boats, you could make enough money in a year to buy two more, then you would have five boats. Three years after that, you would have enough for ten boats."

"Why would I want ten boats?"

"If you had ten boats, you would be the richest guide in the whole village," said the Mountain Climber.

The Freedom Fighter interjected, "With that kind of money, you could do whatever you want!"

"Thanks, but no," said the Craftsperson. "What I want to do is fish all day and feed my family. And I'm doing that already."

In a strong partnership, the partners share a *common goal* for the business. Broadly speaking, you should choose partners in the same category as you. This means you first need to self-assess to determine which of these three categories you belong to. You can perform this self-assessment by honestly answering three questions.

The first question is: Why do I want to be in business? Mountain Climbers want to be in business to attain wealth and status. Freedom Fighters want to be their own boss and make enough money to do the other things they want to do. Craftspeople want to be the best at their work, not for the status, but just to know they're the *best*. Mountain Climbers who make shoes want to build the next Nike. Freedom Fighters who make shoes do as a means to gain financial independence so they can enjoy their leisure time. Craftspeople simply want to make the best shoes possible.

The second question is: Do you want to join a country club or buy a cabin, and why? Mountain Climbers might join a country club for the status and contacts, but hardly ever play golf. A cabin would be a waste of time, but they might have a second home in the sun. Freedom Fighters might join a country club because they enjoy the golf and the pool. They might buy a cabin for the quality family time away. Craftspeople do not want to join a country club or buy a cabin, unless it helps them be better at their craft.

The third question is: Why do you want to be rich? Mountain Climbers want to be rich because they view their net worth as a measure of success. Freedom Fighters want to be rich so they can spend time on their outside interests. Craftspeople want to be rich so they can pursue their craft without worrying about money.

You should find a partner who is motivated by the same values as you are. Mixing types can be hazardous, especially if there are only two or three partners. Mountain Climbers will be frustrated when their Freedom Fighter partner leaves work at 6:00 every night to have dinner with her family. Craftspeople and Mountain Climbers will be frustrated by their different attitudes towards risk, and also by their different attitude towards the product. Craftspeople want to make the *best* products. Mountain Climbers want to make the most *profitable* ones. Freedom Fighters want to reach a point where the business can run well while they're away, but Craftspeople want to control every aspect of the product. At their core, each of these types has an expectation of how a business should be operated. All of these attitudes are *reasonable*, but they're often *incompatible*.

To determine the category your potential partner fits into, simply repeat the exercise with them. Have them honestly answer the same three questions. If their answers are similar to yours, you may have a potential partner.

The Rest of the Story

In August 2017, the Court ordered judgment in excess of $2 million against Minuteman and in favor of their largest vendor and creditor, the King George Company, because Hessian had withheld their payments.

Hessian breached the Share Purchase Agreements and violated the law in its treatment of Madison and Adams, and they lost millions as a result. Madison and Adams eventually sued Hessian, and two years later, reached a substantial settlement. However, they endured much pain and expense in the five years of working with and suing Hessian, all of which could have been avoided if they had been more careful about selecting their business partner.

Section II

Chapter 5:
Habits

I n the early 1970's, John Mondati and James Sheehan founded
Villa Maria, Inc. to build and operate a nursing home[25]. Mondati
handled the money and Sheehan had the operational expertise. This seemed like a good match.

At the outset, Mondati contributed the land for the facility, and
Sheehan agreed to arrange financing for construction and operation. The partners made all the right agreements. In addition
to clarifying their roles, the agreement also contained a buy-sell
provision governing how the business would be valued if one
party wanted to sell his shares. Sheehan and his brother held two
board seats, while Mondati and his attorney held the other two.
Mondati served as President, and was charged with operating
the company.

As agreed, Sheehan arranged financing in the amount of
$650,000. He and his brother personally guaranteed the loan,
plus additional financing to purchase beds, office equipment, and
furnishings, and to provide operating capital. Mondati arranged

---

25 *Matter of Villa Maria, Inc.*, 312 N.W.2d 921 (Minn. 1981).

for Uptown Pharmacy, a corporation of which he was the sole owner, to provide drugs and merchandise on credit, and provided smaller loans from friends and relatives.

Unfortunately, the buy-sell provision was based on Book Value instead of Fair Market Value. "Book Value" is the value on the balance sheet. It is the total depreciated asset value minus intangible assets (like patents and goodwill) and liabilities.[26] On the other hand, Fair Market Value is the price that an asset would *sell* for on the open market. [27] These values are usually different, because the deduction of depreciation and intangible assets doesn't match the actual impact these values have on the amount a buyer would pay.

In our case, Fair Market Value was much higher than Book Value. This difference gave Mondati, as president, leverage to acquire Sheehan's shares for less than Fair Market Value.

Problems arose because Sheehan did not know Mondati as well as he should have. It turned out Mondati was a poor communicator and avoided confronting problems.

Mondati's habits of poor communication and avoidance soon became evident. He managed the company without regard to Sheehan's interest. He failed to communicate important matters, took action without consent of the directors, and held no annual meetings of the directors or shareholders. Mondati did not

---

26 Kenton, Will; Book Value
   https://www.investopedia.com/terms/b/bookvalue.asp.

27 Chen, James; Fair Market Value
   https://www.investopedia.com/terms/f/fairmarketvalue.asp.

share financial statements with his partners. He refused to even consider possible ways to finance dividends. When Sheehan asked for a special meeting, Mondati avoided the confrontation by refusing to attend. Although Sheehan had used his credit to obtain considerable financing for the corporation, he received no return on this investment.

Mondati refused to issue dividends, but instead sought unsuccessfully to buy Sheehan's shares, offering double the book value. Although twice the value he was *required* to pay under the Buy-Sell Agreement, this amount was still substantially less than the Fair Market Value of the shares. Sheehan declined to sell.

Mondati arranged to have another of his companies buy the land adjacent to Villa Maria's facility, then *lease* it to Villa Maria for use as a parking lot. Mondati concealed its availability and acquisition from his partners. Mondati also received offers to purchase the nursing home, which he never communicated to Sheehan.

Mondati's conduct revealed his general attitude toward the nursing home. His failure to consult Sheehan when making decisions or to hold annual meetings (or attend when special meetings were called) precluded Sheehan from taking any part in the corporation. Sheehan was effectively frozen out of the business and had to take Mondati to court.

Most poor partnership communication is not as blatant as Mondati's. It's a warning sign if you have difficulty getting important information, like financial statements, or your partner refuses to consult you on core business matters. Avoidance behavior, like not holding or attending meetings, is also a red flag. Bad habits like revising history and destructive behavior are also clear warning signs that there is a problem to be addressed.

Poor Communication

Strong communication between partners is critical to a strong partnership. You don't need to be best friends, but you *do* need to be open and honest with each other. You must be able to discuss business problems. You must be able to share bad news. You must be able to discuss everything you think and feel about the business. The most common signs of poor communication are a partner hiding information, avoiding issues, and making ad hominem attacks.

When partners hide information from each other, the business suffers. Partners have a right to know everything that's relevant. Hiding relevant business information is often a sign of hiding something else, like an addiction, a mistake, or even a crime. When you ask your partner for financial details, they should come quickly and without objection. Most hidden information is more subtle than cheating on the financials.

Partners tend to hide mistakes using the rationale that it's not really material, or not worth bothering about. A common example is a minor mistake with a key customer. A partner misses a deadline, or gets into an argument with the customer. The relationship is bruised, but not broken, and the offending partner is embarrassed to admit the mistake. So he decides to keep the event a secret and fix it himself. Perhaps he even fixes the problem, and the partner never hears about it. However, if partners make a habit of keeping little secrets from each other, soon they're keeping big secrets, and their cumulative weight will be a drag on the business.

Avoidance is one thing to avoid. Avoidance behaviors are any actions a person takes to escape from difficult issues without dealing with them. These behaviors occur in many different ways and may include actions that a person does or does not take.[28] A partner may avoid an unpleasant task, like firing a long-time employee, or facing a difficult customer, so he becomes "too busy," or plans "to take care of it next week." Minor avoidance behaviors, like procrastinating on a difficult call, are common and not of great concern *if* the call is eventually made. However, avoidance is a sign of poor communication. When it becomes common, you must address it.

To paraphrase James Baldwin: not every problem you face can be solved, but no problem can be solved until it's faced. If your partner avoids problems or difficult tasks, these matters remain unsolved and unfinished. Difficult customers become *former* customers, while unproductive employees continue to be unproductive, which extrapolates into a terrible situation. Not every challenge is fun or easy. The margin of success often lies in tackling tasks you'd rather leave to someone else. But if the boss avoids difficult problems, eventually someone else will become the boss.

An ad hominem argument is an attack on the person instead of the argument. For example, imagine you and your partner are

___

28 https://www.verywellmind.com/how-to-reduce-your-panic-related-avoidance-behaviors-2584148#:~:text=Avoidance%20behaviors%20are%20any%20actions,does%20or%20does%20not%20do.

discussing the best approach to a new customer. You suggest inviting him to play golf. Your partner responds by saying, "You *always* want to take them golfing." Even if he's correct and you have a bias toward customer golf, the partner has not addressed the question at hand: whether taking this customer golfing is a good idea. Thus, golfing with this client is taken off the table without really considering whether or not it was a good idea. Ad hominem attacks are doubly destructive. The problem remains unaddressed and the attacked partner feels frustrated, resentful and angry because his idea was not considered.

Ad hominem attacks carry their own markers. Whenever the argument addresses the person instead of the problem, it's an ad hominem attack. When you hear generalizations like, "you always," "he never," and "they all," it's a sure sign of an ad hominem attack (unless the response is, "I know this guy, and he never golfs"). Just because the person with the idea is stupid doesn't mean the *idea* is stupid. An optimist who believes things will eventually work out, might be right. A politician who's just spewing the party line might still be supporting good policy. In the end, the message is more important than the messenger. Focus on the problem you're discussing and avoid ad hominem attacks.

Poor communication is a bad habit that can sink a business. The right way to communicate with your partner is to be honest, candid, and open. If you and your partner have trouble communicating in this way, it's a sign you might not be good partners.

Revisionism

Revisionism is the toxic combination of dishonesty and avoidance. Revisionism is the changing of history to justify the actual (usually disappointing) results. A revisionist is trying to pretend a bad result is actually acceptable. The revisionist may be trying to deceive others or himself. It's dishonest either way. Revisionism allows one to avoid problems by pretending that no problem exists. The issue is that the problem is ignored and, therefore, not solved.

Revisionism manifests in making excuses or blaming others. "I was counting on Fred to get me that report," is both an excuse and a blame. Perhaps you really were relying on Fred, but if you're the boss, the responsibility is still yours. To be clear, Fred did not fail to give the report to his boss; his boss failed to *get* the report from Fred. If Fred is not reliable, the boss's mistake was relying on him. If Fred did not understand the assignment, it's because the boss didn't make the assignment clear. Bosses get the credit, and must also take the blame.

Sometimes, revisionists simply lie. A revisionist might say, "I never promised it by Friday," even when he did. This signals a problem with honesty. If your partner is revising history in this way, this is a clear warning signal.

Revisionism can take the form of changing goals to fit results. If your sales goal was $1 million and you only hit $800,000, you need to figure out where the problem was. "But $800,000 is a pretty good year, anyway," does not solve the problem. You may have been too optimistic in your forecast. You may have relied on development of a sector that didn't develop. Whatever error caused you to fall short of the goal, you need to address it. Otherwise, you'll keep repeating the same mistakes.

Self-Destructive Behavior

Personally-destructive behavior can often lead to business-destructive behavior. Addiction, unchecked, is likely to take down a business as the addiction becomes more important to the partner than the business. The cycle is common. As the addiction consumes the partner's life, he gives the business less and less attention. His performance suffers. He misses a deadline or blows a sale. Then another. He spends less time working. The mistakes continue. His contribution wanes. Before too long, he becomes a burden to the business. If the addiction takes over completely, the business itself could be destroyed. If your partner has addiction issues, then you need to deal with them as soon as you recognize them.

While recognizing substance abuse takes many forms beyond the scope of this book, it's important to have *some* idea of how to recognize a substance-abuse problem in your partner. The Center for Disease control states, "One group typically in need of early intervention is people who binge drink: people who have consumed at least five (for men) or four (for women) drinks on a single occasion at least once in the past 30 days," and "people who use substances while driving, and women who use substances while pregnant."[29]

A partner with a gambling problem can quickly destroy a business. Signs of compulsive gambling disorder include, among others: being preoccupied with gambling, such as constantly planning how to get more gambling money; trying to get back lost money

---

29 https://addiction.surgeongeneral.gov/sites/default/files/surgeon-generals-report.pdf.

by gambling more (chasing losses); and lying to family members or others to hide the extent of the gambling. Unlike most casual gamblers who stop when losing or set a loss limit, people with a compulsive gambling problem are compelled to keep playing to recover their money — a pattern that becomes increasingly destructive over time.[30]

According to Stanford Children's Health,[31] there are four stages of addiction:

Experimentation

Alcohol or drug use starts with experimentation or voluntary use. In this stage, the use is infrequent and, in the case of teenagers, the substance is usually obtained from and used with friends in response to peer pressure.

Older people who start to use drugs or drink heavily often do so in response to problems in their lives, such as losing a spouse or a job.

Some people in this stage are able to stop using by themselves. Others, however, who believe their substance abuse is solving their problems, or making them feel better, begin drinking more alcohol or taking more drugs, moving on to regular use.

The use of alcohol or tobacco products by legal-aged adults is socially acceptable and does not usually constitute abuse unless

---

30 https://www.mayoclinic.org/diseases-conditions/compulsive-gambling/symptoms-causes/syc-20355178.

31 https://www.stanfordchildrens.org/en/topic/default?id=stages-of-substance-abuse-1-3060.

they escalate to problem or risky use, or dependence develops as described below.

Regular use

This stage is characterized by use on a regular basis. The person may continue to use with friends or acquaintances or may use the substance while alone. Regular use does not have to be every day, but is sometimes continued use in a predictable pattern (every weekend) or in predictable circumstances (when lonely, bored, or stressed).

Problem or risky use

During this stage, the user begins to suffer legal, emotional, physical, or social problems. Adults may drink and drive, or have problems at work or in relationships. Teenagers may have bad grades, behavioral problems, and a significant change in friends, motor vehicle crashes, or speeding tickets.

Dependence

Someone who is dependent on drugs and/or alcohol will continue to use these substances regularly despite the harm their use is causing, including bodily changes causing altered reactions to the substance.

The characteristics of dependence include:

·   Chronic use of alcohol or other drugs that leads to failure to fulfill major responsibilities related to work, family or school.

·   Repeatedly drinking or using drugs in situations that are hazardous, such as driving.

- Development of increased tolerance to use, meaning more of the drug or alcohol is needed to have the same effect.

- Withdrawal symptoms if a person cuts back on use.

Addiction

At this stage, substance use is compulsive and out of control. Addiction is a medical condition involving psychological and physical changes from repeated heavy use of alcohol, other drugs or both.

The primary symptoms of addiction are uncontrollable alcohol or other drug craving, seeking and use.

If you or your partner is suffering from addiction, you should seek help from a health care provider or substance-abuse professional. If you ignore it, you're practicing avoidance. And you are putting the business at risk.

Bad Habits Can Sometimes Be Fixed

A partner's bad habits do not have to mean the demise of the business. These habits are warning signs that you have a problem to deal with. Of course, there's risk in confronting a business partner with his own bad habit. But there is also risk in doing nothing.

Most partners are not actively trying to destroy their own business. If you candidly address the problem in the early stages, it's possible that the bad habit can be repaired. On the other hand, if your partner is actually trying to harm the business for his own benefit, it's best to bring that out in the open as soon as possible.

You must deal with bad habits in the early stages. If your partner is displaying any of these bad habits, you should strongly consider taking action to prevent further harm.

The Rest of the Story

When the problems at Villa Maria became too severe to ignore, Sheehan brought suit to remove Mondati as president and dissolve the company. The Court concluded that Mondati used his position as president to run Villa Maria in his own interest, and in doing so, he acted unfairly toward Sheehan. As a result, the Court dissolved Villa Maria and ordered Sheehan be paid Fair Market Value for his shares. Sheehan waited too long to deal with the problem and ended up in court, but at least he was able to eventually obtain the value of his shares.

Chapter 6:

Traits

I n 1985, Harvey Grimm and his wife, Arlene, incorporated Winton's, Inc. to acquire and operate a motel in New Ulm, Minnesota. Mr. Westgor, who was the Grimms' broker on the purchase of the motel, received 17% ownership of the motel in lieu of his brokerage commission. The Grimms later regretted taking on Westgor as a partner. Westgor was not really part of the business operation, but he was an owner. Westgor objected to the way the Grimms operated the business. He eventually took them to court.

The New Ulm motel was a full-time job for both Grimms, and still struggled financially. They operated the motel for five years, staffing the office and cleaning the rooms, sometimes without a paycheck. Finally, they decided to sell. The Grimms used $30,000 of the cash down payment to pay themselves back wages. Westgor objected to this payment.

Westgor demanded Harvey Grimm sue the attorney who had advised liquidation of Winton's Inc. at the time of the sale of the motel. Grimm refused to liquidate and refused to sue the lawyer. Liquidation would have had severe adverse tax consequences for the corporation, so the Grimms decided to keep Winton's, Inc an active corporation.

After selling the motel, the Grimms, as Winton's, Inc., obtained a franchise to sell Wausau homes. Before too long, the Grimms decided that Winton's, Inc. should abandon the Wausau home business, and sold the company's model home to the Grimms' son, Charles. Charles made payments on the principal balance, and Winton's, Inc. paid all the expenses associated with the home for two years after the sale. During that time, Winton's, Inc. used the home as an office, and the Grimms sometimes lived there. Westgor (who still had a 17% interest in the corporation) objected to this arrangement.

The Grimms and Westgor did not get along. He wanted to cash out of Winton's, but the Grimms could not afford to buy his shares. This led to stress, disagreements and eventually the courthouse.

Warning Signs

Certain traits in a partner indicate future problems that can lead to disaster. You should strongly reconsider being in a partnership with anyone who has trouble managing money; who does not do their job well; who is a cheater; or who is irresponsible. These four particular traits are signs of potential major problems.

Finances

If your partner can't handle their personal finances, they will not be able to handle business finances.

One of the most common problems in partnerships is a partner who treats the *business* funds as if they were *personal* funds.

A partner should never take cash from the business informally. Each partner who works in the business should take a regular salary, paid as part of payroll. Funds available as profits should be distributed through formal distributions as approved by the Board of Directors. In this context, "distributions" is a term of art. A distribution is a release of available profits from a business to its owners at the end of each year (sometimes quarterly) which the owners have decided are not needed for the continued operation of the business. This does not mean that $100,000 in cash available at year-end should always be distributed. Distributions should be decided upon as part of the annual budgeting process, and should only be taken from the company when it's clear that the company will not need the funds for normal operations, or for potential growth.

Signals demonstrating a partner is bad at handling money are most obvious in their personal financial management. A partner who has excessive personal debt can hurt the business because they may need more cash than the business justifies paying them. If your partner has a car you think is beyond their means, this may be a sign of a problem. The same is true if a partner is "house poor," living in a fabulous house, but having trouble paying the mortgage.

Whenever your partner uses company funds to pay for personal expenses you should immediately address the issue. Many business owners carry a company credit card to pay for business expenses. These credit card statements should be reviewed monthly as a matter of course. Personal expenses paid with company credit cards should be a rare event, and should be reimbursed by the partner as they are incurred. If a partner doesn't have sufficient funds on their personal credit cards to pay for a personal expense, perhaps they can't afford the expense. Use of a company credit card for personal expenses is an early sign of personal financial trouble for a partner.

If your partner is regularly overspending company budgets, this also indicates a problem with financial management. Budgeting should be done annually, reviewed quarterly, and strictly adhered to. Of course, there are exceptions. Any spending over budget should be discussed between the partners. Exceptions should be made only when the business operation justifies doing so. If this happens regularly, then there may be a problem with the budgeting process, or with your partner's ability to handle money. Either way, you have a problem that must be addressed.

Bad at the Job

If your partner is bad at his job, it's bad for the business. While this may seem obvious, it's often ignored. People frequently become partners because they're old friends, or share a common interest. They trust each other. However, if your partner serves in the role as chief financial officer, but is not skilled at finance, it will create problems for the business. If one partner is skilled at sales, but the operations partner cannot get the orders filled, the business will suffer. Ask yourself this question: friendship, ownership, and trust aside, would I hire this person to do this job?

If your partner is not good at the job they're assigned, there are potential solutions. One solution is to obtain training for them so that they can perform better. Another solution is to hire an employee who can do that job and create appropriate alternate assignments for the partner. No one person possesses all the skills necessary to operate a successful business. However, successful businesses have skilled people in every important position. Therefore, if your partner is not skilled at their job, you need to get them help, or get rid of them. Whether they can be trained to handle the responsibility, or another employee can do the job better, must be decided in each situation.

Cheating

A cheater will cheat at anything. If a person cheats in one area of their life, they will likely cheat in others as well. If a player cheats at golf, they will cheat in business. Corollary to this rule is that if a person will cheat for small amounts of money, they will cheat for large amounts. If your partner cheats on his wife (or life partner), he will cheat on you (his business partner).

You should be wary if your partner is dishonest in small things. If your partner gives the cashier a ten-dollar bill, but the cashier returns change for a twenty, does your partner correct the error? If he doesn't, this is a bad sign. Its seriousness becomes evident when we more closely examine why he didn't correct the error.

Your partner doesn't need the extra ten dollars, so why did he keep it? He kept it, likely, because he felt *entitled* to it. A cheater believes that if another party's mistake or incompetence benefits him, then he can rightfully take advantage of that situation. This extends to more important situations. He will also believe that treating his family vacation as a business expense is okay, if he doesn't get caught. A cheater doesn't feel remorse for cheating, only remorse for being caught. This means that you cannot trust him. You must scrutinize every penny he spends, review all his credit card statements, and watch everything he does, because he will take advantage if you don't. This is not a road to a successful business or a strong partnership.

When I was in college, my friends and I played a dice game. We played it so often that we had each reached the same skill level, and the game had become less interesting. So we made a new rule. The new rule allowed players to cheat, and they would be punished only in the game—not morally—if they were caught. Thus, we were all free to *try* and cheat without fear of damaging our friendships or trust for each other. This changed the game entirely, and required exceptional diligence. In short, it made the game much more difficult and more interesting to play. This variation to our game doesn't work in partnerships. Cheaters do not feel morally obligated to play fair. As in our dice game, cheaters are not ashamed to be caught. They pay the price and hope to get away with it next time.

Irresponsible behavior

You need to trust your partner not only to be honest, but also to be responsible.

Be wary of irresponsible behavior. This includes missed appointments, absenteeism, and lack of preparation. It also includes making excuses or blaming others for poor results. Responsibility is an adult trait. Irresponsible behavior shows not only immaturity, but also indifference to the success of your business.

A partner who consistently misses appointments or breaks commitments (even minor ones) is being irresponsible. Next to family, your business should be the most important thing in your partner's life. Of course, events sometimes arise that make it necessary to miss appointments or other commitments. If you think your partner might be missing commitments to the point of irresponsibility, you should employ the Frequency and Magnitude Test.

In the Frequency and Magnitude Test, you look at how often your partner is missing appointments (frequency) and the importance of those commitments (magnitude). A partner who misses one weekly sales meeting in the course of twelve months is not a problem. The frequency is low, and the magnitude of a weekly meeting is also low. On the other hand, a partner who misses half of the weekly sales meetings might be a problem because of the high frequency. On the other side, a partner who misses a single *important* meeting without a strong explanation, might be irresponsible. A second time a partner misses an important meeting, the issue should be discussed. If your partner is frequently breaking minor commitments or occasionally breaking major commitments, this may be a sign that you have an irresponsible partner.

Perhaps the most obvious manifestation of responsibility is showing up. It has been said that 50% of business is showing up, and the other 50% is being well prepared. An irresponsible partner might come to work late, leave early, or too often, not show up at all. Or he may come to the meeting unprepared. After years of practice, many business people can fake their way through a routine meeting. However, doing so creates mistakes and missed opportunities. It's simply irresponsible not to show up or to show up unprepared. If this happens regularly, you should find out why.

Another facet of irresponsibility is not taking responsibility for your obligations. When you're the boss, an employee's mistake might not be your fault, but it *is* your responsibility. You cannot blame the employee who gave you bad information, even if they did. When things go south, if your partner blames others, this is a warning sign.

Blaming others provides an excuse to fail. Often, business success depends on closing the major deal or maintaining relationships with an important, but difficult, client. Difficult challenges require extra effort, and often extra effort beyond that. The drive to succeed is what keeps us going in these hard situations. If your partner does not take responsibility for the potential failure, then he may not have that extra drive it takes to successfully handle difficult situations. Sometimes, the first sign of an irresponsible business partner is avoiding difficult situations, even minor ones. Partners with poor communication habits, like not returning phone calls, or responding to e-mails, are demonstrating irresponsibility. If your partner is exhibiting poor communication skills, you should examine the situation to see if there are other warning signs.

Running a successful business is difficult. It's harder if your partner's bad traits are getting in the way. A partner who does not handle money well, cannot do their job well, cheats, or is irresponsible, makes it less likely the business will succeed. If your partner has any of these traits, you should address the situation and either fix it or consider leaving the partnership.

The Rest of the Story

Westgor actually sued the Grimms, claiming that the payment of their back wages, their refusal to sue the lawyer, and the sale of the model home to their son Charles, were all breaches of the Grimms' fiduciary duty to Westgor. Westgor lost in court and appealed. The appellate court sent the case back to the trial court on one issue. That decision was appealed again. Finally, eight years after the lawsuit started, the Grimms won the case.

There is no record of how much the Grimms paid their lawyers, or the emotional toll of the extended lawsuit. To be sure, it was an expensive and troublesome venture. The Grimms' mistake was they had a business partner with a bad trait: Westgor was not experienced or skilled at *any* aspect of the business. He was a passive investor, which might have worked if he had expertise in *some* passive aspect, like finance, hospitality, or real estate. Presumably, the Grimms saved money at the start by converting a cash brokerage fee to Westgor's ownership. But by picking the wrong business partner, this decision cost them far more than it was worth.

Chapter 7:
Differing Values and Vision

I n 1985, Gerald King and Barnaby Miller formed Summerhill Supplies, Inc. to manufacture plumbing supplies. King and Miller each owned 40% of SSI. The remaining 20% was owned in small amounts by seven other investors. All went well until 1997, when a difference in the owners' values led to a disagreement, then to some bad acts, and finally a courtroom brawl.

From the beginning, Summerhill Supplies was a member of its local trade association (LTA). Members were encouraged to contribute to the trade association's Political Action Committee (PAC). Summerhill's CEO and partner, Gerald King, observed this unwritten rule, and annually made his contribution. King was a political agnostic, and viewed the contribution as part of the price of the many benefits the trade association provided the company. President and partner, Barnaby Miller, was passionate about certain political issues, and disagreed with King's contribution. Miller refused to contribute, but King's contribution satisfied the unwritten rule, and the company thrived.

At one point, the LTA PAC began using its funds to support candidates whose stand on certain issues was morally repugnant to Miller. Miller demanded that King stop the contributions because he was morally opposed to candidates supported by the LTA, while King insisted on contributing, for pragmatic business reasons. Even as Miller's complaints became more strident, King believed the LTA was good for business. Both men were genuine (and stubborn) in their positions. This difference created a division between the partners, which grew until it became an impassable chasm.

The Board of Directors was comprised of King, Miller, and one designee of the minority membership group. As the divide between King and Miller grew, this third board member became the swing vote as the dispute between Miller and King spread to other issues. Eventually, King and Miller could not agree on anything.

In 1998, Miller asked the Board to remove King from his office as CEO. The Board found no cause to remove King, but that didn't stop Miller from trying.

Miller persisted. He offered King a carrot in the form of a buyout package, but King refused. Miller then swung a stick by introducing a motion to reduce King's salary by 50%, which also failed. Miller then tried to convince the Board to amend SSI's Bylaws to prohibit political donations, but that maneuver failed as well.

The whole operation of SSI was dependent on its manufacturing plant. Miller realized that if he could somehow seize the plant, he could effectively get rid of King and his LTA friends. Miller had one more parliamentary trick up his sleeve.

Under the bylaws, Miller figured out a way to go around the third board member who had repeatedly stymied his takeover attempts. SSI's bylaws provided that the company could sell real estate if (1) Owners of at least 50% of all shares agreed, and (2) the sale was for Fair Market Value, as determined by a qualified appraiser. This vote by the owners, instead of the Board, made Miller's plan feasible. Miller's group included his forty percent, and two other owners who held six percent each. These two owners did not hold enough equity to create a majority needed to appoint the third Director, but they were enough to put Miller over the 50% threshold to sell the real estate.

Miller remained as President of SSI, but also created a new, secret company, called Winterstorm Supply, Inc. The secret company included Miller and the two minority investors who supported his moral position. Winterstorm drafted Articles of Incorporation, a Control Agreement, and Bylaws. Miller became President of Winterstorm, and then had an attorney prepare a warranty deed conveying the SSI manufacturing plant to Winterstorm. He also hired a friendly appraiser, who opined on the Fair Market Value of the manufacturing plant at around 50% of its actual value.

Miller concealed all this activity from King and the other SSI owners, while retaining his position as President. He never told King, or the other SSI officers, of his plans. Miller also encouraged the other two members of the Winterstorm group to remain quiet.

Finally, on November 13, 1998, Miller informed King that he intended to seek approval to sell the manufacturing plant at the annual meeting two days later. At the annual meeting, a motion was put before the ownership. The Winterstorm group, as holders of a majority of shares, voted to sell SSI's real estate to Winterstorm at the (lowball) appraised value.

Four days after the annual meeting, Miller, as President of SSI, executed a warranty deed, transferring the plant to Winterstorm. Winterstorm moved into the plant and changed the locks. Winterstorm hired all the SSI employees and began manufacturing its own brand of plumbing supplies. They sold to SSI's customers, because SSI could no longer fill its orders. King and the other investors were left out in the cold.

This is an example of how a difference in values can lead to the demise of a business. It was reasonable for King to make a pragmatic political contribution because it helps the business. It was also reasonable for Miller to oppose contributions to causes he considered immoral. Perhaps they could have worked out their problems with better communication. But the crack became a canyon, and before long, the atmosphere became so acrimonious that the partners couldn't discuss anything.

Business partners who have incompatible core values or company vision will eventually run into this problem. They can avoid trouble if the partners agree on the core values, and vision of the business, at the very beginning.

Differing Values and Vision

It is critical to the success of a partnership that the partners share the same predominant set of values and vision for the company. As concepts, values and vision are cousins, but they did not grow up in the same town. Both value and vision are created using the principles that a business deems important, but are distinctly different concepts.

Values

"Values" are the principles that guide the operation of the business. Is it more important for the business to be sensitive to its impact on the environment, or to save money by using components that are cheaper, but not as environmentally friendly? Does the company believe that overpaying its employees creates better employees, or that employees are essentially fungible and should be paid as little as possible? Does the character of the people you do business with matter, or just the customers' ability to pay?

In a small business, the values of the business usually reflect the values of the principals. If you're not willing to do business with a racist, and your partner *is* willing, then you may have problems. In the SSI example above, the demise of the partnership arose because of differing principles of its leaders. In that case, the differing values of the leadership were so personally ingrained and immutable that there was no room for compromise. When partners have such deep-seeded beliefs that oppose each other, there will eventually come a time when compromise is not possible. A women's health clinic with two partners would have difficultly operating if one of the partners believed in a woman's right to choose, and the other believed that abortion should be illegal.

I had a client, Allison, who was a 50% partner with a man, David, who was (to be kind) from the "old school." David believed that women were generally compromising and that if a deadlock arose, he could overrule his female partner. This stereotype fooled him into believing he could take on a 50% female partner and still have full control of the company. Allison, however, was smart, well-educated, and a fighter.

Early in the partnership, David asserted control in subtle ways. When Allison resisted, he was unable to discuss the issue with the open mind that partners need. Instead, his sexism and pride made it impossible to "lose" an argument to a woman, even if she was right. Their issues were centered on common business problems, like budgets and finance. Allison expected an equal partnership, but David could not function as an equal working with a woman. Tensions eventually escalated, lawyers were hired, and the company was dissolved. I'm happy to say that the resolution was a fair buyout of Allison's interest, which she used to start her own business in competition with her former partner.

In this context, values refer to bedrock principles. Each of us have things that we would not compromise on. Most people are not willing to cheat on their taxes, but some are. Most people in the 21st century will not discriminate in employment, or their customer base, on the basis of race, religion, gender or sexual preference, but some do. Often, neither party is inherently wrong; they just believe different things, but those differences can make it impossible to run a business as partners.

Vision

Vision is the partners' idea of what the company will be in the *future*. Partners with differing visions will have constant arguments about strategy and tactics. As with values, differing visions do not necessarily mean one or the other partner is wrong, they just want different things.

You can think of vision as the partner's projection of the company five or ten years into the future. If one partner wants to make a nice living, and then sell the company for enough to fund an early retirement, that partner will want to employ certain strategies. If the other partner wants to *grow* the business into a global conglomerate, he will use different strategies. Another partner might want to operate a business where he doesn't have to work overly hard, can enjoy time with family, and does well financially. There are similarities between vision and business purpose.

In our chapter on business purpose, we discussed the three types of entrepreneurs. To refresh, *Mountain Climbers* want to take on every challenge. Their vision for the company is that it becomes a huge enterprise, and the money is just a way of keeping score. A *Freedom Fighter's* vision for the company is that the business should be successful enough to support their other hobbies and interests. The Freedom Fighter will be more risk-averse than the Mountain Climber, and will be more open to sell the company when a legitimate offer comes along. The *Craftsman* cares little about money, except that he needs to make enough to continue doing what he loves. The Craftsman just wants to make the *best product*, and is not interested in growth for its own sake. These different types of business partners have different visions for the company.

Differing visions means different strategy. A Mountain Climber will be willing to accept more risk and more debt to grow the company. A Freedom Fighter may take on some debt, but will want to see a quick payoff. A Craftsman is more risk-averse, and rarely willing to incur debt. While the actual risk associated with debt is the same for each, the reward is different. The reward for the Mountain Climber is more employees, more customers, and more revenue, and ultimately fulfilling the Mountain Climber's vision. For the Freedom Fighter, more employees just means more stress, which may be worthwhile if the payback is ample. For the Craftsman, more employees and more revenue are not rewarding at all. They are burdens. The Craftsman would rather spend his time making the best product than thinking strategically about finance and layers of management. None of these visions is inherently wrong. If the partners agree on the vision for the business, any of these visions can work. It just depends on your definition of success.

Mission Statements and Vision Statements

Your business needs direction. A bickering couple driving their rental car in an unfamiliar city can get lost because they don't know where they're going, and they do not know how to get there. Likewise, every business should have both a Mission Statement *and* a Vision Statement agreed upon by all partners.

Establishing a Vision Statement forces the partners to determine the business's destination. It also creates a set of principles for the company to operate by. Your Vision Statement describes where you see the company in five or ten years. It's a concise explanation of the organization's long-term objectives.

A **Mission Statement** describes the organization's overall *intention*. It defines your business *purpose* and your *approach* to reaching your objectives. The Mission Statement supports the vision and serves to communicate purpose and direction to employees, customers, vendors and other stakeholders. Mission Statements come in many forms, and you can find examples all over the Internet.

If partners cannot work through differences to determine the mission and vision of the company, it's a sure sign of problems ahead. Your company's strategic plan is steered by the Mission Statement and Vision Statement. Without these, your strategy is rudderless.

Questions to consider when drafting mission statements could include:

- What is our organization's purpose?

- Why does our organization exist?

- Who do we serve?

- Where do we operate?

A **Vision Statement** looks forward and creates a mental image of the ideal state the organization wants to achieve. It is both inspirational and aspirational. It should challenge employees.

Questions to consider when drafting vision statements include:

- What problem are we seeking to solve?

- Where are we headed?

- If we achieved all of our strategic goals, what would we look like ten years from now?

- How many employees do we want?

- What's our big audacious goal?

Building a Mission Statement and a Vision Statement is a good early test of whether partners are suitable for each other. Partners must be able to agree on fundamental questions like "What is our company's purpose," and, "Where are we headed?"

The first sign that your partnership might be in trouble is often finding out that your partner has bad habits, bad traits, different values, or a different vision than you. This will often manifest itself in small ways. However, there are times when these problems are so obvious they cannot be ignored.

The Rest of the Story

Miller's maneuver gave him effective control of the business, but King and the other SSI partners had some options. They took Miller and Winterstorm to court, alleging breach of fiduciary duty by Miller, and other claims against Winterstorm. The court held that Miller's scheme violated his fiduciary duty, and he lost his ownership in SSI. The court nullified the sale of the manufacturing plant, but let SSI keep the money it had received for the sale. Winterstorm was ejected from the manufacturing plant. Both Miller and Winterstorm were found liable for damages, and forced to pay all of its revenue to Summerhill Supplies.

We can only imagine the confusion this caused among suppliers, employees, and customers, and the ultimate damage to SSI's reputation in the community. All of this could have been avoided had the partners been in alignment on their vision and values.

Chapter 8:
Red Flags

I n the 1980's two cousins, Richard Quill and Charles Malizia, formed a partnership to buy and develop real estate. The cousins, along with Charles's wife, Ann, jointly purchased and developed several pieces of Delaware real estate. During a contentious break up, the cousins were unable to reach a resolution on one of their properties, known as the Palmer Property. In the end, they had to go through a trial to determine ownership. Although no one saw it at the time, the dispute was predictable.[32]

The cousins had an informal arrangement. Richard and Charles first went into business together in 1990 by forming Rodney Street Associates, a Delaware Corporation, and purchasing property in Wilmington through that entity. Later that year, they refinanced that property through a formal loan with a mortgage from Charles's father, Ernest, thus beginning an ongoing relationship with Ernest, who served as financier of some of their endeavors.

The Palmer Property became available in 1994. Richard and Charles signed a contract to buy it, and made two non-refundable

---

32 *Quill v. Malizia*, 2005 WL 578975 (Del. Ch. Mar. 4, 2005).

deposits of $1,000, and $14,000, from the joint checking account used by the cousins for their joint endeavors. After paying the deposit, the cousins sought financing to complete the purchase, but without success. So Charles once again turned to his father, Ernest.

Prior to closing, the purchase agreement was changed. Ernest took title *in his own name,* paying the outstanding purchase price of $138,000, and *reimbursing* the cousins their combined $15,000 deposits. Charles attended the closing, but Richard did not. The issue of what the change in buyer was meant to accomplish was hotly disputed. To complicate matters, Ernest passed away, so he couldn't clarify his thoughts in the dispute.

Richard had to sue Ernest's heirs over ownership of the Palmer Property. Charles had given him a Red Flag, but Richard failed to see it.

A Red Flag is any strong signal that one partner might be putting his own interest above the partnership, or acting inconsistently with the partners' expectations. Charles's unilateral deal with his father to buy what Richard *thought* would be a *partnership* property, was a Red Flag. When Charles put Ernest in title to the Palmer Property, there's no doubt that Richard *should* have been consulted.

Property acquisition is a major partnership decision. The partners had always decided together what properties to buy or not buy. The equal partners should both have had input into the decision about Ernest's role in the purchase. When Charles made this decision without consulting Richard, Richard should have been alarmed.

It's possible that Charles was doing what he thought was best for the partnership. The cousins were not in position to close the deal, and stood to lose their $15,000. By bringing in his father, Charles rescued the $15,000 deposit for the partnership. The Red Flag was not Charles bringing in Ernest; it was doing so without consulting his partner.

A Red Flag is action by one partner that clearly demonstrates the problems with Habits, Traits and Values discussed above. Generally, a Red Flag will reveal the existence of more than one issue. For example, if a partner suffers a large gambling loss, it may reveal both the destructive behavior and a bad financial history. Charles's unilateral action reveals the habit of poor communication, and perhaps a differing vision for the property.

A Red Flag *indicates* a problem, but doesn't prove one. If you see any of the Red Flags in this chapter, you should closely examine the situation with an objective eye. If you find that the Red Flag reveals serious problems with Habits, Traits or Values, you should consider whether this partnership is still strong.

Unilateral Action

If your partner takes unilateral action, it's a clear sign that you might have a problem. Unilateral action, when one partner acts without informing or consulting his partners, comes in many forms. The most common forms of unilateral action are taking a distribution from the company, borrowing money on behalf of the company, or entering into a major contract for the company. It's true that each of these can be a legitimate business act. However, none of these serious steps should be done by one partner without first consulting with all partners.

I had a client named Diana, who I helped buy into a business with an older man, Thomas. Diana bought 50% of the company, with the mutual plan being that she would buy the other half over the next five years, at which point Thomas would retire. Diana and Thomas were nominally equals in the company. They were the only two board members. Diana was President and Thomas was CEO. Things went smoothly for a few months.

About 90 days after she came into the company, Thomas unilaterally fired Diana. Like most companies, the President and CEO could be terminated by the Board, but the only two board members were Thomas and Diana. However, Thomas claimed that Diana could not vote regarding her own employment as President, so, as the sole board member eligible to vote, he could fire her. His plan was to make life so miserable for her that she would sell her half of the company to him on the cheap, just to get out. He enjoyed litigation, and thought that Diana would have to sue him to regain her employment, but his plan had a flaw.

Under their agreements, the Board had to be chosen by the owners, and Diana still owned half the company. So, Thomas was powerless to remove her from her board seat. The legal principle called "The Goose v. Gander Rule" says that if a rule is applied to one partner, then it will be applied the same way to all partners. The day after Thomas fired Diana as President, Diana employed the Goose v. Gander Rule, and fired him as CEO.

Their angry lawyer called me and demanded Diana reinstate Thomas, because there was no one left to run the company. I agreed that the situation was dire and ridiculous. At our insistence, both Diana and Thomas were reinstated. Buyout negotiations commenced, and thirty days later Thomas paid Diana a premium for her ownership.

A partner taking unilateral action is usually less obvious. He might enter into a contract without consulting his partner, but then apologize, and claim he didn't have time to ask. He might take money out of the company, then offer his partner the same amount, so as to appear fair. He might take a loan for the company and claim that the company really needed the financing. In each case, the partner is still taking unilateral action. Even if you would have agreed with him, your partner should always consult you before taking major or unusual action on behalf of the business.

If your partner takes unilateral action and hides it, that's an obvious warning sign that you have a bad business partner. Less obvious, but just as serious, is when a partner takes unilateral action and only tells you about it after the act is complete. Whenever your partner takes unilateral action, it's a Red Flag, and you should seriously consider whether you should stay in the partnership.

Using Company Credit Cards for Personal Expenses

We all have credit cards. Many business people have a card they use for business expenses, with the bill paid directly by the company. This is an efficient way to provide access to funds and track business expenses. It's a useful and ubiquitous business practice. But it can be easily abused.

Business people know that you should never comingle business funds with personal funds. Using company credit cards for personal expenses is a violation of this rule. If your partner is using the company card for personal expenses, it's a Red Flag that she may have personal financial problems.

There are only two reasons one would use a company card for a personal expense. Either the partner does not have personal funds (or credit) sufficient to pay for the expense, or the partner wants *the company* to pay for a *personal* purchase. Both situations are symptomatic of a bad business partner. In the former situation, the partner is living beyond his means and asking you to help him pay for it. In the latter, he just wants you to pay for his personal expenses. In either case, you do not want to be partners with that guy.

Lying or Hiding Information

As discussed previously, good partners are always open and honest with each other. This means sharing good news and bad, triumphs and troubles. If your partner is deceitful, that's a Red Flag.

There is never a good reason to lie to a business partner. Your partner might be lying to hide a destructive trait, like a drinking problem, or he might just be dishonest. You should be *especially* wary of lies about *small* things. A person who will lie about little things will also lie about big things. If your business partner lies to you, your trust will naturally break down. Loss of trust is the beginning of the end for a business partnership.

Hiding problems is another danger sign. If your partner's big client is dissatisfied, you should know about it. His unhappy customer is your problem too. Very few problems can be solved by ignoring them. Good partners work together to solve problems. Trouble partners hide problems form each other.

Be wary if your partner hides things or lies to their spouse. Their spouse is their partner in life. You are their partner in business. Generally speaking, anyone willing to lie to their spouse will also be willing lie to their business partner.

Trust is foundational to a good partnership. Partners need to honor that trust. Violation of that trust is hard to recover. Most businesses do not survive a loss of trust.

Breakdown in Communication

Strong communication is critical to a strong partnership. The most important aspect of strong communication is that partners listen to each other. It's healthy when partners respectfully disagree. It is unhealthy when partners stop listening to each other.

It helps to remember that the point of any serious partner discussion is to decide what's best for the business. The physical act of listening can be difficult. It requires concentration more than anything else. Concentration is easier if you really *care* about what the other person is saying.

We all have days when our concentration is not all there. We get distracted by the other parts of our lives. If your partner appears distant or distracted every so often, it's not a real problem. In such case, if you need her to understand what you're saying, you can just call them out and bring them back to the discussion. This happens to everyone, and is not cause for alarm.

However, if your partner just stops caring about your input, or is chronically distracted, that's a Red Flag. When at work, your partner should be interested in the business. If your partner does not have time to discuss serious issues, or seems chronically distracted, this may be a sign of other personal issues. If you think your partner is chronically not listening to you, you should set aside time to discuss it, perhaps after hours. Openly discussing problems like poor communication is a sign of a strong partnership. Not discussing such issues, and not listening to each other, is a Red Flag.

A close cousin of not listening is the partner who will not *respond*. If you have something you wish to discuss, they should respond to you. If they're too busy, they can at least tell you that they don't have time today. A partner who chronically ignores emails or phone calls may not be paying attention to business. Or they may have another distraction that needs to be revealed.

The Rest of the Story

Richard sued Ernest's estate for half the value of the Palmer House. Richard testified that he thought he and Charles owned the property, and never knew the title had gone to Ernest. He believed that Ernest had provided a *loan* to the Cousins to enable them to close the purchase. Charles testified that there was no contract with Ernest, but at most, an informal, non-binding family understanding that if the Cousins could later arrange their financing, Ernest would resell the property to them at a favorable price.

The court believed Charles. Richard was denied any ownership in the property, which went to Ernest's heirs, including Charles. Had Richard called out the Red Flag (Charles not consulting him) earlier, perhaps the right agreements could have been put in place and the lawsuit avoided.

Section III

Chapter 9:
When It's Time to Go

The Bernie Madoff scandal left a wake of destruction. I became involved in the aftermath. Bernie Madoff was a financial manager who invested billions for clients around the world. For many years, he claimed huge returns, unmatched by any money manager. Unfortunately, these returns turned out to be entirely fraudulent. Madoff was running a Ponzi scheme. Instead of investing his clients' money, he used funds from later investors to pay "returns" to earlier investors. His arrest and conviction led to the largest bankruptcy in the history of the United States. Ultimately, the bankruptcy trustee recovered more than $20 billion for investors.

Madoff was very particular about who he allowed to invest in his fund. He required a minimum of $500,000 in any single payment. As a result, much of Madoff's money came from "feeder funds" where an individual would gather money from other investors and send it to Madoff in the required amount.

Carl was the general partner of a limited partnership that served as a feeder fund. Carl was an accountant who invited four of his wealthiest client families to invest. For years, Carl was able to show huge returns through the Madoff fund, and was the darling of his clients. Then the scam was revealed. When these families found out that all of them, including Carl, were victims of a crime, they saw it as a Red Flag. As Managing Partner, Carl was the target of their wrath.

Carl came to me when his partners sued him for getting them involved in the Madoff meltdown. Carl was also sued by the partners in his accounting firm. In addition, the victimized investors sued the feeder fund. Carl himself was devastated, essentially broke. My first job was to unwind the spaghetti, understand all the players, and develop a plan.

After much discussion and investigation, we developed a plan that involved defending the lawsuits, making counterclaims and taking advantage of the significant power bestowed by the governing documents of the limited partnership.

Under the governing documents of the feeder fund, Carl, the General Partner, had the right to choose the fund's attorney. As General Partner, he had a personal right to indemnity from the fund for action he took. This meant that the feeder fund had to pay attorneys' fees for both itself and Carl. Although the fund had lost $9 million, there was still enough money in the fund to pay for the litigation. This war chest gave us the opportunity to execute our plan.

Carl knew all the opposing parties very well. He had worked in the accounting firm for twenty years, so knew the leadership intimately. The investors in his feeder fund were his most important clients, with whom he had worked for decades. As their accountant, he knew everything about their financial situations. For example, one client had sold his family business for $50 million, but Carl knew that he had already lost almost all of that money on soured investments in restaurants and a vineyard. He knew this client would be motivated by receiving enough money to create some sort of financial security for his children. Carl also knew that the current President of the accounting firm would be motivated not so much by money (he had plenty) but by inflicting pain on Carl. Through Carl's personal knowledge we were able to accurately assess what each of the opposing parties would perceive to be in their own best interest. Certainly, each of them would like to get all of their money back, but this wasn't their main motivation.

At the time of the litigation, the trustee in the Madoff bankruptcy was actively recovering funds for investors, well on his way to recovering more than $20 billion. So our first task was to call a meeting of those who had invested in Carl's feeder fund. In that meeting, we were able to explain the success of the bankruptcy trustee, and share the predictions (from neutral observers) that all Madoff investors could expect to get most of their money back. We were also able to convince Carl's partners, truthfully, that Carl had lost everything, so they would be unable to recover any money from him personally.

Another important part of this meeting was showing them that the feeder fund was rightfully paying the attorneys' fees for both itself and for Carl. The investors objected, but the governing documents were clear. The result of this initial meeting was to deflect the opposition's interest in collecting money from Carl personally. At the end they realized that such effort would be expensive and fruitless, and so it was in their own best interest to wait for the money to come from the bankruptcy trustee, as expected.

With the money issue aside, we still had to deal with the oppositions' main motivation. They wanted to punish Carl for leading them to such disastrous losses. Of course, Carl could not be expected to know Madoff's fund was a fraud. Madoff had been regularly audited and approved by the SEC. Nobody in the public knew there was a problem until Madoff's arrest. To satisfy the investors, and his former accounting partners' desire for punishment, we had to convince them that Carl was not at fault. Our argument made some headway, but no one was willing to let Carl walk away without losing a pound of flesh.

What to do when it's time to separate from your partners.

Business divorces are generally high on emotion. They are the end of an important and close relationship. Usually, one or more partners feels wronged. For at least one of the partners, it means leaving a business they have successfully grown. All of this emotion is amplified by the financial stakes, usually in the millions of dollars. Combining high emotion with high finance means that both sides will fight hard to win the ensuing battle.

To ensure success in a business divorce, it's important to set emotion aside. A business divorce is really just a business transaction with a litigation component. Your leverage in the transaction will be based on a combination of the law, your agreements, and the parties' ability and willingness to sustain a long battle.

Understand your Rights and Obligations

When you find yourself in need of separating from your partner, your first step should be to hire your own lawyer. You will have rights and obligations, both as an individual and as a company. Whether you need to eject a bad business partner, or find yourself being pushed out, the process will be governed by law, and your original company agreements (your Bylaws, Control Agreement and Buy-Sell Agreement) will dictate the process once you decide to divorce.

A lawyer experienced in business divorce can provide options that may not be obvious, and can help you create a plan for solving the problem. Your options are to proceed by taking corporate action, negotiating a deal, or starting a lawsuit. Usually, the solution is a combination of all three. This is your War Plan.

Creating Your War Plan

Preparation of a strategic War Plan vastly improves your chances for success in a partnership break up. You will do better if you know what you want to achieve, and the route you want to take. You'll be able to see around the next corner. You'll avoid making important decisions without full consideration. You'll know when to push and when to walk away.

Decide on your Attitude

Every business divorce has a tone on a scale ranging from friendly to adversarial, and stakes ranging from low to high. You should choose your attitude, ranging from Cooperative to Full Bulldog, based on these factors.

This chart will help you choose the attitude to take depending on the nature of the dispute.

	Friendly	Adversarial
Low Stakes	Cooperative	Tough with some cooperation
High Stakes	Tough with some Bulldog	Full Bulldog

For example, in a friendly, low-stakes dispute, you'll get your best deal if you're *cooperative*. When your attitude is *cooperative*, you share information and work together with the other side to reach a mutually acceptable solution. This does not mean you are passive, or that you give away what you want. A *cooperative* attitude just means that you are trying to work with the other side to find a solution that works for you, and is acceptable to the other side.

In an adversarial, high-stakes dispute, you need to go Full Bulldog. This means you do everything in your power to win concessions from the other side. It doesn't mean that you're always aggressive because sometimes the best way to gain concessions is with finesse. It does mean you prepare a detailed strategic plan and execute on that plan. Never concede *anything*, without receiving something, *anything*, in return. Full Bulldog means you're prepared to litigate. Adversarial, high-stakes situations require strength, finesse and planning. Your goal is to win.

When situations are either low-stakes and adversarial, or high-stakes and friendly, you need to be tough. A tough attitude will include both cooperation and resistance. Tough is hard on the issues, while soft on the people. If you're not tough, an adversarial opponent will run you over and take the low stakes, while a friendly opponent will pick your pocket while he smiles to your face. These situations require that you prepare a strategic plan so you know where to cooperate, and where to resist. You should be wary of an opponent who seems friendly in a high-stakes situation. Remember, people will always act in their *own* best interest, so the opponent in a high-stakes situation who seems friendly may actually be adversarial.

You should determine your attitude at the very beginning. It's possible to change attitudes in the middle of a dispute, but it can be counterproductive. Moving from Full Bulldog to Cooperative signals that you have lost. Watch for this in your opponent. Moving from Cooperative to Full Bulldog is sometimes the right move, but you may have to live with the concessions you offered in the Cooperative phase of the negotiation.

In almost every case, it's best to choose an attitude, and maintain it consistently throughout the dispute. Your War Plan will inform this choice.

Understand Every Party's BATNA

BATNA means "Best Alternative to a Negotiated Agreement," a term coined by Roger Fisher and William Ury in their 1981 bestseller, *Getting to Yes: Negotiating Without Giving In.*

You need to understand what will happen to you and to your partner if you fail to reach an agreement. You gain leverage by simply knowing your partner's BATNA, and by being honest with yourself about your own BATNA, from the very beginning. You can understand BATNA by answering three questions:

What will happen to your partner if no agreement is reached?

Human behavior is predictable, if you understand the person. You know your partner better than perhaps even their spouse. You've seen your partner in times of high stress. You know what makes them tick. You know what scares them. This knowledge will be valuable in developing your War Plan.

If no agreement is reached, what will happen to your partner? Will they lose an opportunity? Will they go out of business? If a lawsuit follows, is this better for you or for them? Explore all your partner's options. The answers to this question will provide insight into your partner's personal motivation. It's one of the driving forces in the negotiation. Think about the individual. Is he capable of operating the business by himself? How does he feel about the status quo? Can he afford a lawsuit?

What will happen to you if no agreement is reached?

You must be honest with yourself about your own alternatives. If you're not honest with yourself at the beginning, you'll pay for it in the end. If you're in a lawsuit and you think you have a great claim, you might overvalue your case, and leave a good offer on the table.

Often, examination of your own alternatives reveals your partner's BATNA. If you were trying to sell Coca-Cola® as the exclusive cola for a concert hall, your product is easily replaceable by Pepsi®, so your opponent has a good BATNA. You must be aware of such alternative positions during the negotiation. On the other hand, if you have no competition, then you can be more aggressive.

It's also important to understand your own motivation. Why are you fighting? Are you trying to get as much money as possible, or trying to make a point? Are you seeking revenge? Are you just defending your own actions?

Can you take action to change either BATNA?

If you don't like the BATNA, either your opponent's or your own, you can take action to change the alternatives.

One way to change BATNA is to change the players involved. There are two components to changing the players. First, you must consider whether there are *extra* players you can involve who will increase your leverage. Second, you must consider who you need to add to your team to execute the War Plan.

Adding players can change the tenor of a business divorce. If your goal is to buy out your partner, and you know his wife wants to move to Florida, then including her in the conversation can be beneficial. She will naturally put pressure on him to get the deal done. If your partner is taking unreasonable positions and does not have a lawyer, sometimes having him hire a lawyer can create a more reasonable negotiation. If you're short on cash, you can bring in a financial partner.

Look for players who will have a significant negative impact on your partner's BATNA. Is there a key employee or client who refuses to work with them? If your partner is stealing, involving the police can make him very cooperative.

You will need to add players to build your own team. Your team must have the education, experience and skills to execute your War Plan. Ideally, every facet of your War Plan will be in the hands of an expert. Examine each aspect of your War Plan and decide who will be responsible for executing it. You will need a lawyer. You may need a valuation expert. You may need an accountant, real estate appraiser or an expert on industry best practices. If you don't have the financial expertise, you need to add someone to your team who does. Of course, the cost of hiring experts can be limiting, but must also consider the risk of fighting without the proper expertise. Hiring the right lawyer might cost you $100,000 in fees, but *not* having one might cost you $1 million on the purchase price. Each person you add to your team should be a net asset.

Another way to change BATNA is by *fait accompli*. You may be able to take corporate action to remove an option for your opponent. Can you remove him from the Board? Perhaps it would be helpful to fire your partner. You can take the dispute public, or perhaps just reveal the dispute to a key customer or employee. You can start the lawsuit. There are many possible ways to increase your leverage. Anything you can do to create more risk or better opportunity for your partner, without harming your own position, improves your relative BATNA.

Prepare Budgets for both Time and Expense

You never have unlimited time or money for a transaction. Preparation helps control costs. You need to know how much time and money you have to devote to the negotiation, and you should also have an idea of the time and money your opponent plans to spend. If you don't budged at the outset, you will be surprised at some point deep into process. These are those moments when you realize, "This is taking too long," or you decide, "Let's just get this deal done." These thoughts do not display impatience; they're indicators of a failure to properly budget the time or money you actually need to complete the process.

Your budget for time and money is crucial in determining your results. Time and money spent in preparation saves many multiples later on. For example, with proper preparation, you'll create the right team up front. If you have to bring in somebody later for a particular issue, someone will have to spend time educating the new member. If you don't have time to fully educate the new team member, their contribution will suffer.

Your partner also has time and money constraints that you may use to your advantage. If you know your partner has a burning desire to retire, you can probably make a lower offer. Like buying a car at the end of the month, you might gain leverage when your partner is motivated to reach a deal. These are both examples of what happens when one party is at the end of their time budget.

Set Your Goals

There's much discussion about the impact of setting goals prior to starting a battle. I have clients who believe that you get the best results by determining your Optimal Reasonable Result, then stretching that position to *start* at an unreasonable point. This is called the "big pot" position. Others believe starting at a reasonable position yields better results.

111

Studies on big pot tactics are mixed, but there's a general consensus that negotiators who set specific but difficult goals tend to get better results. You can use the psychological effect of the "Set Point" to create an advantage. That is, the first number you hear sets the bar for the rest of the discussion. If you want to sell your shares for at least $5 million, and your initial ask is $6M, then $5M will seem like a bargain. Many negotiation experts will suggest, "Don't ask for what you want; ask for the most you can *justify.*" If your goal is to sell your shares for at least $5 million and your partner's goal is to buy for the best price she can get, the sale price will probably be at least $5 million. On the other hand, if your goal is to sell the shares for as much as you can, and your partner's goal is to buy it for less than $5 million the sale price will probably be less than $5 million.

Your goals should be achievable. That's why you set them only after you understand everyone's BATNA and you have set your time and money budgets.

You should set your goals in terms of a *range* between the number at which you will walk away from any deal (your "minimally acceptable outcome") and the best you could reasonably hope for (your "optimum reasonable outcome"). This is the range in which you can expect to reach an agreement, if agreement is possible. Then you need to assess your partner's position. By examining their motivation and BATNA, you can establish their *minimally acceptable outcome* and *maximum reasonable outcome.*

The overlap between these two ranges is the Deal Range. If agreement is possible, it will fall in this range. With this information at hand, you then can decide, strategically, how you want the negotiation to proceed. Are you better off taking a big pot position and negotiating down? Or, should you start with a more reasonable position? An aggressive position at the beginning is less likely to lead to an agreement, but also likely to give you a better outcome if an agreement is reached.

Of note, if the two ranges do *not* overlap, that means you need to change somebody's BATNA. If you can't find a Deal Range, then you will probably not be able to negotiate an agreement. This means your War Plan will start with a lawsuit or other stronger action. Factors that might justify a higher or lower valuation include: assumption of debt, accounts receivable, inventory, real estate, leases, tenant buildout, machinery, furniture and fixtures, tax liability, accounts payable, supply chain good will, key accounts, intellectual property, growth trends, competitive environment, and merchantability of the business. Other items to consider: precedent, non-compete agreements, employment agreements with key employees, special licenses, and the final payout structure (cash v. annuity).

In one case, John had been fired from his job as President by his partner, Betty, the CEO, but he remained on the Board. We were able to create significant personal risk for Betty by taking advantage of an unusual provision in their Control Agreement. The provision mandated that the salaries for one partner were to be set by the other partner. In normal times, this provision would balance the two sides, but because John was no longer being paid a salary, his partner had no counter move. We called a board meeting and reduced Betty's salary by 50%. This changed her BATNA and led directly to a generous payment for John's shares.

With your War Plan and your team in place, the only thing left is execution of the plan. The best advice during execution is to stick to your budgets, be flexible when circumstances change and expect a dogfight.

The Rest of the Story

Carl's partners wanted to punish him for investing in Madoff's fund. To find a potential agreement that would minimize that punishment, we had to assess the Deal Range. In most cases, the Deal Range is set in terms of money or contractual agreements. Carl's case was different. The main variable was how much punishment would be doled out to Carl. The investors' initial offer was that any money the bankruptcy returned to Carl would go to them. We knew this was not about the money, but about punishment, and was a "big pot" position.

One of our advantages was that the remedies available to the opposition in litigation were actually quite limited. Under the assumption that the Madoff victims would be made whole by the bankruptcy trustee, a long lawsuit would result in Carl paying nothing, because the investors would not have suffered damages if they got their money back. In addition, Carl's attorneys' fees were being covered by the feeder fund, and the investors were paying their *own* fees, so we knew they had no interest in protracted litigation. Also in our favor was that the opponents were Carl's former friends and business partners. Therefore, we expected their animus to evolve into a more empathetic position as time passed, and they understood that Carl was as much as a victim as they were.

Based on all this, we decided that Carl would not offer money, but would be willing to forgo his partnership benefits from the accounting firm, and would be willing to reimburse the feeder fund (and thus the investors) for the attorneys' fees paid by the feeder fund. Our initial big pot position was that, based on the inability to recover anything in litigation, Carl would pay nothing, and simply litigate. Everyone knew the parties had to come together to negotiate. As a group, we decided to enter a grand mediation, using a former judge as mediator, who had gained a reputation for solving difficult and complex disputes. When I brought his name up to opposing counsel, they were glad to have him. Because of his reputation for resolving such matters, their quick approval led me to believe that they were motivated to resolve the matter.

We believed the investors would require Carl to suffer some sacrifice, but given their BATNA (fruitless, expensive litigation) we believed they would not demand too much. We set the Deal Range between simply giving up Carl's partnership benefits (which we believed was the minimum they would require) and Carl keeping funds the bankruptcy trustee recovered for him (our optimal reasonable outcome).

The mediation began with the parties in six different conference rooms at the mediator's law firm. The first session lasted two days. No agreement was reached, but progress was made. Negotiations continued through the mediator for three months. In retrospect, I believe the mediator intentionally used this time to provide seasoning. The investors needed time to recover their empathy for Carl. We emphasized Carl's financial problems whenever we had the chance. Three months after the mediation began, we finally reached agreement. Carl was not required to pay any money, all claims against him were released, and he released his claims for wrongful termination from his accounting firm, giving up his partnership benefits. Carl did not have to reimburse the feeder fund for his attorneys' fees.

The main reason for this successful outcome was Carl's intimate knowledge of the opposing parties. We knew what they wanted, we knew what they needed, and we knew what motivated them individually. Understanding this enabled us to predict their actions and execute a successful War Plan.

Chapter 10:
Timelines and Tactics

enry was the operating partner in a radio station, and had been in radio for 40 years. His financial partner, Ron, had no experience, and was supposed to be passive. Each owned 50% of the station, but Ron was causing problems. He seemed to be working at making life unpleasant enough so Henry would sell him his share of the station. Ron challenged every decision Henry made, and injected himself into the station's operation. Ron also threatened litigation, a baseless claim. Finally, Henry agreed to discuss the sale of his shares and hired me to negotiate the sale of his ownership to Ron.

As we prepared for the negotiations, I considered which players to add to our team. We added an appraiser, who valued Henry's share of the station at $1.2 to $1.4 million. Henry lived a modest lifestyle and didn't really need all the money. He just wanted to get out of the unpleasant situation and retire, so he was willing to sell his ownership for less than full value. However, he was *not* willing to let Ron steal the station.

It's generally a good idea to lock in your key employees as you prepare for sale, but not in this case. Here, the two key employees were Henry's son, Jim, who was the Program Director, and Henry's daughter, Allison, who was the Sales Manager. Jim and Allison were the two most important employees at the station, and completely loyal to their father. They *were* willing to continue to work for Ron, but both had decided that they would not work for him if he didn't treat their father fairly.

After two months of negotiations, Ron had only offered $750,000, well below the acceptable range. We all decided to have one last meeting with Henry, Ron, and the lawyers to see if we could reach an agreement. We met in a conference room for this final try. It was clear to everyone that if an agreement couldn't be reached at this meeting, then the negotiations would be over, and the undesirable status quo would continue.

After several hours of fruitless discussion, Ron and his lawyer asked if Ron could speak with me privately. We went into a smaller conference room and stood toe-to-toe.

"This is Henry's last chance," Ron began.

"I have a final offer to make. I will never offer more than $900,000 for this radio station. Before we go back in that conference room, I want you to tell your client that I'm going to come in with the last and final offer. It will be $900,000. If your client doesn't accept this offer, then we're done."

Ron was playing the "Two Futures close." He was giving Henry two choices. He believed Henry would prefer to take the money rather than get mired down in two years of disruptive litigation. I knew $900,000 was not enough. I also knew that once the "final" offer was made, Henry would either have to *reject* it and face

118

litigation, or *accept* it and move on to a happy retirement. If these were his only choices, Florida looked pretty good, and $900,000 is better than a poke in the eye.

A business divorce is going to take time, effort and emotional energy. One of the key aspects at the beginning of a business divorce is to understand and accept that it will take from 12 to 24 months to resolve, sometimes longer. A partner going through a business divorce should just assume it will take two years, and not expect anything faster than that. Acceptance of this reality provides the patience to enable you to properly plan and achieve the best result possible.

It's important to make constant progress throughout the dispute. Without constant progress, according to a plan, the timeline can extend much farther.

Phase One - Months 1-3: Planning and Setup

One you have decided to leave your partner, the first thing you should do is talk to your lawyer. As discussed above, the lawyer will help you develop your War Plan. Not unlike construction of a building, the War Plan will be a series of planned actions extended over many months.

The timeline suggested here is typical, but all cases are different. The timeline can be accelerated in some cases and sometimes takes longer for a particular stage.

The first three months should be used to provide information to your team and to develop your War Plan. Depending on the complexity of your situation, developing a preliminary plan can take up to a month. Then it can take up to two more months to refine and finalize your War Plan.

In your War Plan you will decide which boardroom tactics to use. Do you want to make a capital call? Do you want to fire your partner? Do you want to give notice of a potential derivative action? You should consider all available weapons and decide which ones to use.

Somewhere in the latter half of Phase One, you will take action that either directly or implicitly lets your partner know that divorce is coming. Sometimes this is a radical action at a board meeting. Sometimes it's a demand letter. Sometimes the first move is terminating your partner. Whatever your first move is, it will signal the end of the first phase. You have finished your planning and moved into execution.

Phase Two - Months 4-6: Negotiation and Commencement of Litigation

Phase two is the negotiation and pre-litigation phase. This is the opportunity to reach an early settlement of the case, if one is available. The best way to achieve an early settlement is by tsunami.

The First Move

Ideally, your first move will create a wave of such overwhelming force that your partner sees resistance as futile and just wants to negotiate a deal. There are a number of tactics that are useful:

Capital Call

If you have significantly more wealth than your partner, you can gain leverage by making a capital call. If you have personal funds available to meet a capital call and your partner doesn't, you can gain leverage by making a capital call.

To justify a capital call, there must be a business need for the money. This can be a desire to pay off debt, to upgrade your plant, or to expand into new territories. Any reasonable use for the funds can justify a capital call. Most businesses can find a good use for extra capital, so you can probably find a reason to make the call.

Your founding agreements will dictate the process for a capital call. Typically, you will call a special meeting of the Board. At the meeting, the Board will approve the call and the partners will have 30 to 60 days to invest their share into the business. If a partner does not contribute his share, another partner can make that contribution. The wealthier thus gains extra owner-ship in the company, and the extra control that goes with it. Further, the partner who does not contribute has a smaller percentage of ownership, so the cost to buy out those shares will be less.

This tactic works well for partners who already have control of the Board. Approval of a capital call will always require majority board approval, and sometimes, depending on the controlling documents, a super-majority. If you control the Board and have stronger personal wealth than your partners, making a capital call can be a powerful first move.

Deadlock

Creating a deadlock on a major issue is a form of brinksman-ship. When a board is deadlocked, the company cannot act. A prolonged deadlock is usually not good for business, but it can be good for a partner seeking a business divorce.

One way to create a deadlock is to find a third party who wants to buy the company's physical plant and real estate in a sale-lease-back arrangement. This is a major decision that requires board approval. To create a deadlock, you simply vote the opposite of your partner, so no decision is made. The potential sale-leaseback will affect business planning in multiple areas and in some cases will stir up the employee base. This ongoing planning impairment makes it difficult to do business, and may motivate your partner to sell his shares (or buy yours) at a reasonable price.

Adverse Actions

There are many ways you can take Adverse Action against your partner. In this context, Adverse Action is anything that makes your partner's life less pleasant. Reducing salary, terminating employment, withholding bonuses, threatening litigation, or hiring someone else to do your partner's job are all forms of Adverse Action. In one case, a client's partner claimed that she owed the company $200,000 based on a thin excuse. Ron's conduct towards Henry is an example of Adverse Action by just being difficult to deal with. Whatever Adverse Action you choose, if your partner is unhappy with you, they will be more motivated to reach an early settlement.

Valuation and Offer

Mature businesses should periodically obtain an independent assessment of their enterprise value. If you are planning to divorce your partner, you should obtain a valuation privately, at your personal expense. If this valuation favors your position (buying or selling), a good first move can be to present your partner with an offer to buy his shares (or sell yours) at the valuation price. He will likely obtain his own valuation, but you will have demonstrated that your proposal is serious and that you are prepared.

Closing Without Litigation

If it's possible to reach an agreement without actually litigating, Phase Two is the most likely time to do so.

Fundamentals of Closing

Closing an agreement is like scoring a touchdown—it can only be achieved if everything else is properly in place. The difficult part is to make sure that everything is properly in place.

Once your goal is in sight, then you can look for the opportunity to close. You have to look at several things. Consider whether your partner is fully seasoned, consider the best method for closing, and then detail your endgame strategy. Your partner is ready to close when she is ready to make the decision that you want her to make. These fundamental closing tactics can get you across the goal line without the time and expense of litigation.

Seasoning

The first rule of closing is not to attempt it prematurely. You must wait until your counterpart is ready. Your partner will not close until their motivation level is satisfied, or threatened to the point where they want to complete the deal. This process is called "seasoning." Expert closers know when their partner is ready for closing and how to get there as efficiently as possible.

The term seasoning really means, "The maturing of your opponent's needs." But it's more than that. It's a process by which the negotiator eventually becomes ready to make a decision. It's a combination of the passage of time, consideration of various options, and evolving discussions that eventually create the motivation to reach an agreement.

If you want to reach a deal with your partner, you must think about seasoning. He has to be ready for a major life change. You know your partner is ready to move on, but if you move too quickly, he might decide that he doesn't *really* want to go. This will result in a more difficult separation and a worse deal for you. A sort of courtship ensues where the partners dance around the issue. At some point, you mutually decide to separate.

You don't have to do all of the seasoning yourself. Parties are regularly seasoned by external events or circumstances. Your partner's spouse can be a great source of seasoning, either by pushing for her to retire, or to get rid of you. If you're already in a dispute and early negotiations have been unsuccessful, the course of litigation will supply the seasoning.

Only when a partner is fully seasoned can you proceed to closing.

The Golden Silence

Silence is an underused closing tactic. Silence is a companion of patience. Patience is an acquired skill. The film *Glengarry Glen Ross* (1992) has an amazing scene in which beleaguered salesman Jack Lemmon describes closing with silence. According to Lemmon, he sat at the target's kitchen table for eighteen minutes in total silence until his target finally picked up the pen and signed the real estate purchase agreement.

Silence can mean sitting in a meeting and being quiet for long periods. It can mean a slight hesitation before offering your next position. Or, it can mean waiting several days to respond to an offer.

Silence is an asset. Your partner needs to believe he has either everything he needs or everything he can get. A period of silence reminds your partner that your acceptance of an offer (or your response to the opposing position) is not easy for you to do. You have given his offer deliberate consideration and your decision is a close call. This creates apprehension in your partner. He fears you might walk away from the deal. This fear feeds the Scarcity Pillar of persuasion and incites your partner to agree with your next proposal. This can all be said by saying nothing.

Split-the-Difference Close

The split-the-difference close is used when two parties are close but can't quite come together. One party offers to "split the difference" in an effort to close the deal. Sometimes this works.

I don't like this method because the other party can gain an advantage by simply rejecting your overture, because you have conceded to a new number and they haven't. Artful negotiators can use this concession to bring you closer to their side than your own.

Another disadvantage is that while splitting the difference *seems* fair, there's really no rational justification for meeting your partner half-way. A split-the-difference counter offer may entice you to give up your minimum acceptable position for no good reason except to appear reasonable.

Imagine you want to buy your partners shares for $3.8 million. She wants to sell, but insists on $3.9 million. You're only $100,000 apart. If you offer to split the difference, her next move is simply to decline. The endgame plays out something like this:

Your partner: I've told you that I really can't accept less than $3.9 million. I appreciate that you're willing to pay $3.85, but if that's your best number, I don't think we can do a deal.

You: Well, I'm only willing to pay $3.85 million if it will get the deal done. My highest number is $3.8 million (Note: you have just conceded that your highest number is now actually $3.85, regardless of what else you say).

Your partner: Yeah, but it seems a shame to let the deal go over $50,000. You will make that much in revenue in the first month. However, I understand we each have our own estimate of what my shares are worth. I believe they're worth $3.9 million; and if I can't sell it to you for that price, I will just stick around.

Now you're in a hard place. He knows you are willing to pay $3.85 million. Your partner is probably willing to take $3.85, but is obliquely threatening to walk away. After some more conversation in which you test her resolve, the discussion sounds like:

You: I will pay you $3.9 million; I will pay $3.8 at closing, and the rest in two payments on the first and second anniversaries of closing.

Your partner: Okay, we have a deal. (Note: you just agreed to pay his price)

If you decide to use the split-the-difference close, you have to be absolutely clear that splitting the difference is not only your *last* number, but also *beyond* your last number (say this only if it is true). You must be willing to walk away if the other side will not split the difference. I don't mean you have to pretend to be willing to walk away—you have to actually be willing to walk away if they do not agree to split the difference.

False Withdrawal: The Doorknob Close

The doorknob close is a false withdrawal from negotiations. I learned this closing technique from my father, a broadcaster who began his career as a radio salesperson. The doorknob close is useful in many different situations.

It gets its name from the following scenario: The parties are sitting at the conference room table negotiating a deal. The negotiations grind to a halt. Our side knows that the other side has one more chip left to play. We also know that the other side is not quite fully seasoned. Our side is concerned that if they give up their last chip, it will be rejected and the sale will be lost. So we politely get up and begin to walk out of the room. But when our hand touches the doorknob, we stop, turn back, and say, "Wait a minute, what if...." and then put the last chip on the table. This is a masterful close because buyer's remorse will set in as you walk toward the door and, in combination with the last concession, will often close the deal.

The doorknob close is not restricted to its literal meaning. My favorite doorknob close story comes from an attorney friend. My friend was the lead on the settlement negotiation team in a huge class action lawsuit. Billions of dollars were at stake. As the trial continued through several weeks, the negotiating teams met daily. My friend's firm was local and the opposing team was from out of town. At the end, the opposition used the doorknob close three times in forty-eight hours. As negotiations broke down, the visiting team would declare an impasse, pack up, and head to the airport. Then they would call from the airport with "a new idea to discuss," and the negotiations would continue. In the end, the case settled before the jury came back. My friend went home and burned the clothes she had worn throughout the last seventy-two hours of negotiations.

Two Futures Close

Closing is about getting the other side to make the decision you want them to make. You can often motivate the other side to do this by showing them that their failure to decide has consequences. The two futures close shows your partner two different Avenues to Closing. One future offers the Avenues of Greed or Hope. The other future is the Avenue of Fear.

Assume you are negotiating to buy out your partner. As negotiations have progressed, you have offered $1.65 million. You aren't willing to pay more than $1.75, but you want to get the deal done. As a last attempt to close before the litigation commences, you increase your offer to $1.75 and make it clear that this will be your final offer. You point out to your partner that his choice is to either accept the big check today with all of the good things—spell those out—that go with that. Or he can spend the next eighteen months immersed in litigation, spend $100,000 on his own lawyer and risk getting less than your offer. Framed properly, your preferred alternative will look very attractive.

These are just a few of the many ways to close a deal. If you combine these tactics with the Four Avenues to Closing, you will get your deal done — and it will be a good one!

Corporate divorces are business deals with a litigation component. As a lawyer who likes to litigate and go to trial, I have found that threatening litigation is much more effective when combined with a Two Futures Close. If you just threaten to litigate, your opponent will be deciding between accepting an offer they may not like, or litigating. They have to choose between two bad choices. On the other hand, in a Two Futures Close, you present one good choice (for example, retirement life on a beach) and a bad choice (years of litigation). Given these choices, your partner is much more likely to make the choice you want.

Closing against Separation Anxiety

Closing a business divorce requires overcoming many obstacles. One of the major obstacles is that, no matter how bad things get, one partner may refuse to let go. You cannot close a business divorce without persuading the other side to make a major life change. If your partner is selling, they will be leaving the business that's been a big part of their identity for many years, and also leaving the person they've spent the most time with (except perhaps their spouse). If your partner is buying you out, they're keeping their job, but they're also making a huge investment and moving forward without a teammate who has been with them for years.

The most important thing to remember if you see a partner who is reluctant to close, that the partner's issue is *emotional*. It's an aversion to a large change. This condition is a manifestation of

129

inertia that arises from your partner's fear of the unknown. This problem becomes apparent most often by a seeming inability to get the deal closed, after negotiations have been reasonably efficient. At first, you may think your partner is simply "nibbling"— trying to get a little bit more at the end of the deal. At some point you will accept a final nibble, only to have your partner move the goalpost. You know your partner well enough to know whether he is the type that moves the goalpost at the end of negotiations. If not, then you probably have a "separation anxiety" issue.

There are three strong strategies to use in the face of separation anxiety. The unique circumstances of each situation will dictate which strategy is best. You can present a Two Futures Close; you can put your partner through some more seasoning; or you can chase the goalpost.

Sometimes, the right strategy is to chase the goalpost. Assume that the deal was almost closed, but your partner has asked for *just one more thing*. It can be a term or it can be a small change in the price, or sometimes it's even delayed because "our lawyers don't have the documents ready."

Chasing the goalpost means you accept the latest nibble. Sometimes, giving away that last piece is advantageous because it will allow you to move forward. Often it's a "souvenir ashtray," a deal point that means little to you but much to your partner. Souvenir ashtrays include items like keeping your partner on the company healthcare for two years; letting him keep the three-year old company car that he's been driving; or paying $5,000 in moving expenses. A souvenir ashtray is anything that one party values much higher than the other. If a souvenir ashtray stands between you and closing the deal, you should give your partner the ashtray.

The problem with chasing the goalpost in a separation anxiety situation is that your partner will not be satisfied with just one concession. Giving him the first ashtray is a litmus test. If they really just want the ashtray then they will accept it and close the deal. That should be the final agreement and the lawyer should start preparing for closing. However, if your partner has separation anxiety, they may come up with a *new* demand (followed by more if you let them). If your partner does this, she likely will continue to obstruct closing, sometimes very politely, until you can motivate her to close the deal. To motivate them you must return to the Four Avenues to Closing and do something that creates persuasion, greed, fear or hope in a high enough dose to overcome her separation anxiety.

Rejection of your partner's second nibble is the first step. He will push back that this particular item means much more to them than it does to you and project his own obstruction to closing on to you. He will blame you for getting in the way by refusing to give this little tiny thing.

At this point, it's important to bring their separation anxiety front and center. You will not overcome the separation anxiety until you actually call it out. Name it. I use a very specific technique when doing so.

The Two Futures Close works well in this situation. I will deliver two messages in the same conversation. This conversation is almost always a phone call or face-to-face meeting. Written communication will not overcome separation anxiety. This is a critical conversation.

In the conversation, you will first point out factually (don't cheat the facts) what has happened to prevent closing. You have already chased the goalpost once, so you *remind* your partner of this fact. After laying this groundwork, then convey your conclusion that the partner is experiencing separation anxiety. Point out that these last nibbles are fairly meaningless. That the only thing left to do is close. "We've been negotiating for months. We gave him the first nibble. We are not giving anymore nibbles." Finally, restate your proposal using the Two Futures Close. The Two Futures Close helps him overcome his fear of commitment by showing him that not closing is worse (the Avenue of Fear) and that closing will make his life better (the Avenue of Hope) or give him new opportunities (the Avenue of Greed). Of course, the approach in any particular situation must be designed according to its own circumstances.

What if your partner surprises you?

If your partner is initiating the corporate divorce, then you will only discover it at the beginning of Phase Two. Your partner will make their first move. While the action may come as a total surprise to you, it has likely been well planned by your partner. You should seek out a business divorce lawyer *immediately*. Often, a fast, but well-planned response will put you back in an equal position, or at least help to neutralize your partner's instigating action.

Donna was in an LLC with one partner, Ray. Everything was equal. Each partner owned 50% of the profits, had 50% of the votes, and they were the only two board members. Even their titles as officers were equivalent, with Donna serving as President and Ray as CEO. Donna called me one day to tell me that Ray had fired her as President. There was a provision in the Operating Agreement that said board members could not vote on matters in which they were personally involved, so Ray asserted that only he could vote on Donna's employment. Fortunately, Donna's position as a board member was protected by another provision, so Ray could not remove her from the Board. Applying the Goose v. Gander Rule, we fired Ray as CEO the next day. When his lawyer called me to say that this left the company with no one to operate it, I proposed we reinstate *both* of them and move on. We did. Shortly thereafter, Ray bought Donna out for a generous price.

Once you neutralize the first move against you, you will be at or near equal footing. This will give you and your lawyer time to create your war plan. Sometimes, you can counter with a tsunami of your own and create an outcome that satisfies your goals.

Whether you're on offense or defense, negotiations should commence shortly after the initial moves. These negotiations should never last more than 90 days, preferably 60 days. The partners know each other, so there is no "feeling out." While it may take time to gather some corporate information, finances etc., there is generally no dispute about what happened. Corporate record books and ledgers control the story. Within thirty days the parties should be exploring meaningful settlement options, if in fact a settlement is possible. If settlement is not possible without litigation, then litigation should be commenced. There is no need to waste time. If the lawsuit is going to happen, you should commence it at around the nine-ty-day mark, certainly no later.

Before commencing litigation, you need to consider your partner's attitude towards it. Some busy people enjoy the "sport" of litigation, and will spend money, time and effort because they actually enjoy it. Some business people detest litigation and would rather overpay early to avoid legal fees and distraction. Most business people fall within these two extremes. They understand that the settlement is just a business transaction, and will let the risks and rewards of potential litigation inform that decision, just as the other risks and rewards of a major business action are considered. The litigation is just part of what informs that decision.

Sometimes, the tsunami move is to commence litigation. In such case, the lawsuit will mark the beginning of Phase Two. However, there will still be negotiation and room for an early settlement.

Phase Three – Months 6-18: Litigation, Mediation and Trial

Phase Three commences when the parties become committed to litigation. This does not necessarily happen the moment that the lawsuit is served. There is often a negotiation period (part of Phase Two) after a lawsuit is served. However, at some point negotiations break down and the parties commit to the rigors of a long lawsuit.

Most business divorce lawsuits last from 12-18 months after the commencement of the suit. Once the parties are committed to execute the litigation, there is a flurry of activity at the beginning. After 2-3 months of such activity, the case will go quiet as the lawyers evaluate the evidence they've gathered. Then there is another flurry of activity as the lawyers gather more evidence. In this period of time, the partners and other key witnesses will be deposed. After about 12 months, the discovery period ends. At this point, there is often a motion for summary judgment. In legal parlance, summary judgment is a motion made before the court which essentially says even if all the disputed facts are viewed in my opponent's favor, I still win the case. These motions can add an extra 3 to 4 months to the litigation timeline. Once this motion is decided, if the case is not dismissed, the parties will begin to prepare for trial and enter mediation.

Mediation is the modern-day version of the "courthouse steps." Mediation is generally the last chance to resolve a complicated case. The parties and lawyers understand completely the facts of the case, including their strengths and weaknesses.

A mediator conducts shuttle diplomacy between the parties. If there is any chance to settle a case before trial, it will be at mediation. In fact, my normal position is that if we can't settle at mediation, then we will not discuss a settlement before trial.

If mediation fails, the case will go to trial. Only about 10% of cases go to trial. The effective device of mediation, combined with the extraordinary expense of preparing for and conducting a trial are usually instrumental in closing settlement gaps.

Trial is an all-or-nothing risk. If you settle the case before trial, you will not get your Maximum Potential Result. However, you are also not exposed to your Maximum Negative Result.

In total, including trial, it is not unusual for a business divorce case to take 18 to 24 months from the first time the initiating partner meets with his lawyer. Of course, you avoid this distraction with an early settlement. Because a business divorce combines the elements of board action, business negotiations and litigation, a well-informed business person will take all of the aspects into consideration in deciding when and how to execute a business divorce.

The Rest of the Story

Ron at the radio station had floated a Two Futures Close, hoping to force Henry to choose between continued conflict, or accepting $900,000 for a business worth at least $1.2 million. However, I knew that Ron would face an employee retention problem. Henry's son and daughter would not work for Ron if they felt he had taken advantage of their father's situation. I also knew that Ron needed these key employees to continue the smooth operation of the station. I believe he floated the offer with me *privately*, instead of making it directly, so he could *test* my reaction. This told me that he *would* pay more than $900,000 if I could assure him they would stay.

I responded, "There's something you need to think about before you make your final offer. You need Jim and Allison to continue working after you buy the station. If you don't, the station will fail, and this will be a bad deal for you no matter *how* cheaply you buy it. I've talked to Jim and Allison. I know that they're willing to work for you, but not if they feel you took advantage of their father. So, before you make a final offer, you should compare saving a few bucks to the cost of losing the station's two key employees. Think about it, and meet me in the main conference room with your lawyer in ten minutes."

About ten minutes later, Ron and his lawyer joined us in the main conference room. Ron spoke first, wagging his finger without sitting down.

"We've been talking long enough, and it's time to reach an agreement or stop negotiating. This is my final offer. After I make this offer you will have thirty minutes to consider it, and then it comes off the table. My final offer is $1.2 million. I will not pay a penny more. And the deal is off if your kids quit. You have thirty minutes. This is your last chance." Then he and his lawyer left the room.

Henry turned to me and said dryly, "Well, that's enough. Let's take it."

The key employees agreed to stay on, and the sale successfully closed a few weeks later.

Chapter 11:
Getting the Business Ready for a Divorce

Caring Homes, Inc. (CHI) operated homes for adult men with mental health issues that required them to live under moderate supervision. My clients, John and Cheryl, were a married couple that owned 50% of CHI. Attila and Griselda, also married, owned the other 50%. Cheryl and Griselda were sisters. The four owners comprised the CHI Board of Directors and all worked full time at CHI, serving a role to which they were well suited, Griselda was the President and CEO. CHI had a good business model but it was not performing well because these owners do not get along at all. The sisters did not even speak to each other.

John and Cheryl came to me when Griselda fired them and stopped paying their salaries. This is called a "freeze out" and prevented John and Cheryl from participating in the operation of CHI. John and Cheryl were still owners and still served on the Board, because Griselda could not take that away from them.

John and Cheryl just wanted to sell their ownership in CHI for a fair price. Attila and Griselda were trying to lever the freeze out to buy their shares for far less than fair value. Everyone wanted the same thing: John and Cheryl selling their shares. The problem was agreeing on a price.

We hired a business valuation expert to give us an opinion of the value of John and Cheryl's ownership. He valued the entire business at between $5.5 and $6.5 million, including $2 million in cash, $2 million in real estate equity and $1.5 million in going concern value. Using this report, we were able to justify a value of $2.8 million to $3.2 million for Cheryl and John's shares.

Then we had to analyze the other side's BATNA. If no agreement was reached, Attila and Griselda faced an expensive lawsuit, with the entire business at risk. It would be in their best interest to get back to peaceful business operations as opposed to the current disruptive state. John and Griselda needed an agreement taking John and Cheryl out of CHI so they could operate peacefully.

We needed to set our goals. In this case our goal was to sell for at least $2.8 million. We believed that Attila and Griselda would not pay that much unless they were motivated by something else. We determined that their price point would increase as their risk increased. To get a fair price, we had to increase their risk until Attila and Griselda perceived it to be in their best interest to pay our price.

Business divorce can be disruptive. You need to prepare the business so it is strong enough to handle the combination of a transition in ownership and potential acrimony between the partners. Ideally, you will start the process months before any problems arise. You need to take every step you can to maximize your company's ability to withstand the pressure. You need to take the time to get everything in order, including your finances, agreements and operations.

Obtain a Professional Valuation of the Business

At the very beginning of the divorce (and before that if you are commencing it), you should hire an expert to provide her opinion of the value of the company. This value acts as a peg in the ground, so everyone knows the amount under discussion.

Some Control Agreements require the company to obtain a valuation annually. In my experience, many companies do not follow this directive. If I use such a provision in a Control Agreement, I make sure that any valuation is no longer valid after eighteen months. This avoids fighting over an obsolete valuation that is clearly unfair to one of the partners. If my client is the one on the short end of the stick, we will fight the old valuation on the grounds of fairness. Likewise, if a Control Agreement uses book value instead of Fair Market Value (FMV), we will fight for the FMV regardless of the Control Agreement. Courts are loath to endorse an unjust valuation just because the letter of the Control Agreement (made long ago) says they must. Obtaining a current valuation avoids this problem.

Once you have a current valuation, you can use it to enforce your position. If a current, reasonable value of the company is $3 million, it is difficult to argue that 40% of the company is worth anything other than $1.2 million. But, because the valuation is an opinion, it is subject to argument from the other side.

There are many ways to pick apart a valuation opinion. Many of these are avoided by presenting audited financials (see below), but some are unavoidable. The partners will argue about the cash flow multiple the expert used. They will argue about the certain liabilities or inventory value. Because the valuation opinion relies on the financial statements, a party who wants to argue about the value can usually find some component of those statements to fight about. Ultimately, both sides will hire experts to fight over the value of the company.

The ultimate purchase price will depend on the relative leverage and BATNA of the partners. However, these factors will play out against the expert value opinion(s) in play. You can tilt the result in your favor, and increase your chances of avoiding litigation, by obtaining a reasonable valuation opinion at the very beginning.

Get Your Finances in Order

The single most important factor in determining the value of a business is the financial condition of the company. Mature companies are valued on a multiple of free cash flow with the standard multiple varying by industry. Whether you are buying or selling, you want to have financial statements the partners can trust. If possible, you will want *audited* financial statements performed, going backward for the three years before the start of the divorce. Audited financials are trustworthy, and in turn, will help your valuation expert support his valuation. All the numbers tie out, which means fewer potential ambiguities and less likelihood of litigation. On the other hand, if your expert relies on financial statements that are *not* in order, or do not fully tie out, she will appear less credible. Audited financials also will help you as you evaluate the changes you can make in the operation.

If an audit is not possible, then have your accountant conduct a "review" of your financial statements. A review is a term of art, meaning the accountant conducts an investigation to verify the financials, but not as thoroughly as they would in conducting an audit. A review is less expensive than an audit, and is far more reliable than a standard financial statement, known as a "compilation." In presenting a compilation, the accountant relies entirely on the company books and does not verify the accuracy of the numbers in the books.

Getting your finances in order helps you find and fix potential problems. You may discover that your inventory is too fat, or that you spend too much on ineffective sales trips. You should remove all unnecessary expenses from your books. I had a client who bought a company and discovered that a key employee had been accumulating paid time off for 20 years, and was owed $200,000. This undisclosed liability put the sale into litigation. The seller could have easily fixed the problem before listing the company. His failure to do so cost him dearly.

Many family businesses run personal expenses through the business. Should the company really be paying for your expensive car? Are you writing off vacations with your wife as business trips, because she's the part-time Sales Assistant? Is your nephew a productive employee, or can you replace him with someone better at the same cost? You might slip these past the IRS, but they'll be red flags for the opposing lawyer in litigating the value of the company.

Business divorce lawyers have seen these situations before, and will exploit them to poke holes in your valuation. You should examine your business with tenacity to call out the problems before someone else does. This makes it possible to eliminate the problems before they cause pain.

Get Your Agreements in Order

During the disruption of a business divorce, you want to maintain the key customers and employees that made the business prosper. In a time of transition, customers, suppliers and employees may be tempted to shop around for a more stable company. If these critical players will stay with you through the transition, your benefits will last for years.

Keeping Your Important Customers and Suppliers

Your key customers and suppliers are with you because they trust you will benefit their business. In a disruptive business divorce, this trust is put into question. Customers often use a transition as a time to shop around. Suppliers may look for better contract terms. All partners want assurance that key customers and suppliers will stay with you, because the viability of the company helps the seller get paid. There are several ways to provide this assurance. The most concrete way to keep customers and suppliers is with contractual commitments. You want contracts that are long-term, exclusive or both.

Long-term contracts are for a year or more. Ideally, the contract will have an evergreen clause, renewing automatically unless your customer takes action to terminate it. Another type of long-term contract is based on volume. The customer commits to a certain minimum purchase over a period of time. This commitment ensures that they will stay with you through the contract period.

Exclusive contracts, making you the *only* provider of a good or service in a particular region (or globally), create the same advantage. Your customer's business becomes dependent on you. As a practical matter, they cannot change providers without a major shift in their own operation. Therefore, they're less likely to shop for another provider as long as you provide quality goods and service.

With suppliers, you agree that they will be *your* exclusive supplier. You can get a supplier to provide discounts, price commitments and volume commitments by agreeing to purchase exclusively from them. Stability in the supply chain is always helpful.

The ideal contract for retaining customers and stabilizing suppliers will be exclusive, evergreen and guarantee an ample volume of business for at least a year. Customers will *not* enter into such a contract amidst a business divorce. You need to set up these contracts in advance.

Often, customers are willing to commit to a long-term or exclusive contract in exchange for discount pricing. While such discounts often make sense, there may be less costly ways to achieve the same outcome. Before approaching your key customers to ask for these commitments, you need to understand their BATNA. Understanding BATNA means understanding what will happen to you, and to your customer, if you fail to reach an agreement. You gain leverage by knowing your customer's BATNA, and by being honest with yourself about your own.

When you understand BATNA, you will be able to find benefits your customers and suppliers gain when they commit to long-term, exclusive contracts. If you can obtain such commitments, you will increase the stability of the business over the course of the divorce.

Keeping Your Important Employees

Your key employees are the engine of your business. You want to know that the people who make your business soar will still be there after the divorce. Employees will stay if they have non-compete agreements, long-term contracts, or financial incentives.[33]

Most employees, especially customer-facing roles like sales, expect to sign non-compete agreements. Also known as restrictive covenants, these agreements will prohibit your key people from competing with you, from soliciting your employees to another company and from doing business with your customers. In total, restrictive covenants discourage your key employees from leaving. Absence of non-compete agreements make your key employees attractive to your competitors, especially during an ownership transition.

If your key employees, especially sellers, do not have restrictive covenants, you should put them in place as soon as possible. To be enforceable, restrictive covenants must be of reasonable time and within a reasonable geographic area. With current employees, you must also give them some type of *consideration* in exchange for the new restrictions. Consideration can be anything (a used car, in one case), but must be something the employee is not otherwise entitled to receive. For example, a discretionary bonus

---

33 I have intentionally excluded "culture" and "personal loyalty" from this list. Culture often changes when one owner leaves and loyalty only goes so far.

can satisfy this requirement, but a performance-based bonus they've already earned does not. Adding restrictive covenants to existing employees requires a legally-intensive analysis, so you should consult a lawyer to implement this change.

Another way to retain employees is with long-term contracts. You give up your right to terminate them at will in exchange for a commitment that they will stay with you for the long term. Your employee gets job security in exchange for giving up their ability to leave the company. When both you and your key employee have no thought of separation, entering into a long-term contract is a win for both sides.

Long-term contracts work well with senior executives, but not as well with sellers and middle-managers. Senior executives already feel a strong emotional bond with the business that most sellers and middle managers do not. There's a risk among the latter group that their motivation will flag when they know they have full job security. Before giving any employee a long-term contract, you should be certain that they're part of the "family" and personally invested in the success of the business.

The third way to motivate employees to stay is by creating long-term financial incentives. These incentives include phantom stock programs, profit-sharing that vests over years, and Employee Stock Ownership Plans (ESOP). These are complex programs, the details of which are beyond the scope of this book and should only be implemented with a lawyer's help. What all such programs have in common is they pay employees based on the long-term success of the business, but only if the employee stays with the company. An employee considering a new position will think twice before walking away from money that she will be paid if she stays for two more years.

Long-term incentive programs can be used to reduce the sting of implementing new non-compete agreements. Employees love these programs. They gain a sense of ownership. There's a world of difference between announcing that you are giving employees a new long-term bonus plan (which will require restrictive covenants) and announcing that you are requiring employees to sign restrictive covenants in exchange for a small payment. The new incentive program will serve as the required consideration of the non-compete. At the same time, your business becomes even more stable because your employees are motivated to stay by both a carrot (long-term financial incentives) and a stick (restrictive covenants).

Get Your Operations in Order

When you live in a house for 20 years, you stop noticing the worn carpet and old paint. The same thing happens when you live in a business for a long time. You've done things your way and you've been successful. But you may have stopped noticing the old software or worn cubicles. The stress of a business divorce will be amplified by little problems in the operation, so you should get rid of the little problems.

The first step in getting your operation in order is easy. Clean and update your premises. Make it look pretty. Get rid of the scrap metal in the yard. Resurface the cement on the shop floor. Paint the building. Employees who work in a clean and well-organized facility will have a higher tolerance for change. On the other hand, if the facility is disorganized and looks dumpy, employees will be less tolerant of the disruptions caused by the divorce.

The second step is more complicated. You should examine your operation in detail and take care of any problems you find. Update your information technology. An IT system that is fully efficient, secure and easy to work with gives employees assurance that the company will get through the turbulence. Get rid of any products, employees, or systems that create drag on your operation, even your pet projects. It's often helpful to bring in a consultant who can look at your operation with an outside eye. They'll find things you overlook.

Taking these steps will minimize the inevitable disruption of a business divorce to your business and your own life. It will make a difficult time a little smoother.

The Rest of the Story

In order for John and Cheryl to get a fair price for their CHI shares, we needed to increase the risk for Attila and Griselda. We accomplished this in two ways. First, we needed to create deadlock on the Board, which would permit us to sue for court-ordered dissolution. Second, we could create significant personal risk for Attila and Griselda by taking advantage of an unusual provision in their Control Agreement, which mandated that the salaries for one couple were to be set by the other couple. In normal times, this provision would balance the two sides, but because John and Cheryl were not being paid, Attila and Griselda had no counter move against them.

149

Attila and Griselda were the buyers, but they had not prepared their business to sustain a difficult divorce. They had not considered their own BATNA, had not put the business in order and had not obtained their own valuation opinion. As a result, they were not in a position to withstand our strategy.

We executed our strategy by calling a special meeting with three agenda items: (1) Reinstatement of employment for John and Cheryl; (2) Disbursement of $2 million in cash held by CHI and (3) Determining salaries for the coming year. The meeting went well. As expected, the first two motions resulted in a 2-2 tie. This created the deadlock we needed, by law, to start a lawsuit that could put the entire company at risk of dissolution.

Then we set the salaries for Attila and Griselda at 50% of their prior salary. This created a personal financial crunch for them. As we left the meeting, I provided the buyers' lawyer with a written proposal and the Business Valuation. We asked for $3.2 million, which we believed would be at the high end of the deal range, assuming our motivational tactics were effective.

Our next step was to wait. Attila and Griselda needed some seasoning. They had to get used to the idea that we controlled their income and that their entire company could be at risk. Several weeks after the meeting, Attila and Griselda's lawyer called me and offered to buy John and Cheryl's shares. We negotiated a purchase price of $3 million.

After the payment was made, Cheryl reminded me that the call from the buyer's lawyer came two days after Attila and Griselda had to make the semi-annual real estate tax payment on their home. Clearly, a personal financial crunch motivated them to close the deal.

Chapter 12:
Finding Money to Buy out Your Partner

"**H**ey Bulldog, I need some grease," came Dan's voice over the phone on a summer Sunday evening. I was out on the deck grilling burgers, so I was confused. I wondered how Dan knew I was grilling, and why would he want one of my burgers?

"Money!" Dan corrected me. "I want to buy out my partner and I need some working capital. Can you help me find some?"

This made more sense. Dan and his partner, Lee, ran a specialty manufacturing plant; fabricating and replacing custom parts for heavy equipment. A typical order might include a machine delivered on a wide-load flatbed needing replacement of a part that weighs hundreds of pounds. Dan and his crew would offload the machine with their crane, find the faulty component, then repair or replace it. Dan's team was very good. They were well-respected in their industry. They never lacked for business, until COVID-19, that is.

Dan owned 75% of the business and Lee owned 25%. They operated a profitable business before COVID and expected to be profitable afterwards, but the shutdown of many plants they served meant that customers did not need to have their equipment repaired. The customers also had their own cash flow problems, so many had to slow-pay their invoices. Revenue was down to almost nothing.

The company was in a precarious position. They had expanded their plant a few years earlier and owed the bank $4.5 million. The payments were easy to cover in normal times, but the pandemic had made these payments difficult. With no work, Dan and Lee were considering laying off employees they did not want to lose. They also owed money to suppliers for inventory that was going nowhere any time soon. The business was on the edge.

Like many partners, hard times exposed the difficulties in Dan and Lee's relationship. They both knew that the vast majority of small business failures are caused by a shortage of cash. Dan wanted to press forward, borrow money and survive the crisis. Lee, on the other hand, was afraid the business would fail and could not stomach the stress of operating without cash reserves. Lee offered to sell his shares to Dan for $500,000, far less than they were worth a year before the pandemic. Dan wanted to seize this opportunity to obtain Lee's shares at a bargain price, but he didn't have the funds to do so.

Cash flow is the life blood of any small business. The right financing can make the difference between your success and failure. There are six basic types of small business financing that all businesses must understand.

Almost *any* business can obtain *some* type of financing to buy out a partner. The cost of the financing is directly related to the credit worthiness of the business. A business that doesn't actually need financing can acquire funds inexpensively. On the other hand, a business in trouble may only be able to borrow money at higher cost.

Payments Over Time

The ideal way to finance your buyout is to pay your partner over time. In a typical seller-financed transaction, you will pay some cash, perhaps 10 to 20% of the purchase price, at the very beginning, then make low payments, perhaps interest only, for three to five years, with a balloon payment due at the end. Seller financing usually carries a low interest rate. The seller will agree to these terms because she wants out of the business and knows the business does not have the cash to pay all at once. She wants the business to do well, because that's the source of her payments. If the finance terms hinder the company's operations, she might not get paid.

In buying out your partner, your first choice should always be to pay your departing partner over time. This works best when your partner is motivated to leave the business. If your partner approaches you about a buyout, your proposal should be to pay 10% down, interest only for five years, then a balloon payment at the end. From there, you can negotiate a deal that pays your partner but does not hinder the business operation.

Traditional Bank Financing

If your partner insists on cash, the first place to look for financing is your bank. Traditional bank financing, including the Small

Business Administration (SBA), is available to businesses with strong credit, but probably will not fund a business divorce. SBA rules require the money be used for certain business purposes, and providing funds to buy out one of the owners is not among them.

I regularly advise clients who are doing well to set up an operating line of credit (LOC). The LOC is a safety net in case of a sudden reversal. The cost of a line of credit is nominal and the business can use as much or as little of the money as it needs, thus saving interest costs as well. It just sits there, helping you to sleep at night. The best time to seek financing is *before* you need it.

An LOC is like a fire extinguisher. You may never need it, but it can save your life. One client, Tammy, saw revenues dropped 50% when her anchor customer stopped ordering. She had an LOC that bridged the gap while she replaced that revenue. My client, Wayne, had a great business until the 2009 recession, and ended up in bankruptcy because he didn't have a safety net. So get a LOC approved while your credit is still strong.

Traditional bank lending is tightly regulated. Bankers have little discretion over who they can lend to. If your business falls within the bank's requirements, financing can be acquired at the lowest cost. In some cases, banks will not even require the owner's personal guarantee. This is the first place a company should go to find financing.

However, if your business falls outside of the minimum credit requirements, you won't be able to obtain a loan. Playing golf with the banker won't help. They must follow their regulatory parameters. However, if your bank won't help you buy out your partner, there are other sources.

High-risk Bank Loans

If your business can't meet the tight regulations at your bank, you may still be able to acquire financing from certain institutions that have a higher tolerance for risk. This option still requires good credit and a good operating history. These lenders will demand a higher interest rate and very high security for the loan. They will uniformly require a personal guarantee.

These lenders are a good place to go if you need a bridge loan, a one-time need for capital to carry you through to a known, upcoming cash event. For example, if you already have a huge order to be delivered and paid for in 90 days, but you need the money now, you could use a bridge loan. I helped a client with a bridge loan so her construction business could complete a big project, and she repaid it when she was paid for the work. In the entertainment industry, festivals, concerts, and films use bridge loans to finance the expense of getting the show ready, then pay it off after the tickets are sold.

Buying out a partner is a one-time cash need. However, there is no significant revenue to offset the cost. Therefore, you will have to show the bank that you will have extra capital because you no longer have a partner. His role in the operation can be replaced by an employee at a lesser salary. In addition, you can keep your income stable and pay the bank with the money that would have been your partner's year-end dividend. After the bank is paid off, those dividends will be yours.

More risk for the lender means more cost for the borrower. High-risk bank lenders are still on the risk-averse end of the spectrum. The cost of this financing will be higher than traditional banks, but less than other categories.

Asset-based Lenders

Now we're getting to the expensive sources of capital. Asset-based lenders will lend you money if you can secure the loan with hard assets. These can include inventory, real estate, accounts receivable, or work in process.

Tim imported plastic lawn furniture from China. He had a large order that he knew would be held up in port unless he paid for it in full. He needed $600,000. Knowing the shipment would create $1.4 million in profit, he borrowed $600,000 from an asset-based lender. Three months later, he repaid the lender $750,000. Very expensive money, but it made sense to pay the $150,000 in finance cost to generate that $1.4 million in profit.

You can use an asset-based lender to buy out your partner if you have assets to secure the loan. Asset-based loans will be over-secured by the hard assets, sometimes up to 200% of the amount of the loan. They will require a personal guarantee. You will also pay a very high interest rate and a significant origination fee. For example, Tim borrowed $600,000 and paid another 25% of the loan in finance costs over just a few months. This high price may be worth paying, if it gets you over the temporary problem. For Tim, it saved a profitable order and helped him prove himself to a large customer.

Factoring

Factoring is a special form of asset-based lending, enabling a company to get fast cash for their accounts receivable (A/R). In a factoring relationship, all accounts receivable are assigned (factored) to the lender. The business issues invoices to its customers, but the customers make payment directly to the lender. The lender will advance funds on the billed, but not yet collected, A/R. When the customers pay the lender, the lender deducts the amount owed, including interest and fees, then transfers the remaining funds to the business. The lender will advance perhaps 50 to 60% of the total A/R before the accounts are paid. The lender will charge a high interest rate and fees for this service.

The obvious advantage of factoring is that it accelerates payment of a company's invoices. For example, if a company issues $1 million in invoices on June 1st, it might receive $500,000 in cash in June, and the rest (less factoring fees and interest) when the invoices are actually paid.

Factoring is a business form of payday loan, where earned-but-uncollected funds can be accessed before they are collected. As with payday loans, it's difficult for a business to break the cycle if they become dependent on factoring. Factoring is appropriate for short-term cash shortages, but can be a problem if the business relies on advances. In addition, a factoring relationship requires your customers to make their payments to a third party, which may reveal your financial difficulties and create a poor impression with the customers.

Factoring is *not* a good choice for buying out your partner. It does not bring in new capital; it only helps you get paid sooner.

However, if the cost of the buyout creates a temporary cash flow shortage, factoring may help you get past that problem.

Hard Money Lenders

A hard money loan is secured by *all* of the company's assets. It is very expensive, including significant origination fees and high interest rates. You can expect onerous terms that favor the lender. I recommend avoiding hard lender owners. Hard money lenders should be avoided, except in the most desperate and temporary situation. This is a very risky arrangement that could end with the lender owning what used to be yours. *Never* use a hard money lender to fund a partner buyout. If your company is in so much distress that you need a hard money loan, it is not the right time to buy out your partner.

For example, Butch owned Big Land Development. Big Land owned a 75-acre parcel of raw land worth about $6 million. Butch took on Dave, a real estate developer, as a partner in Big Land.

Dave was a bad business partner. Without telling Butch, Dave borrowed $1.2 million from a hard money lender. The terms of the loan included a 10% origination fee, a 12% interest rate, and a mortgage on the 75-acre parcel. Within 90 days, Dave had spent almost all of the loan proceeds with no benefit to the development, leaving Big Land unable to service the debt.

Two years after the loan was taken, Butch came to me to defend collection of the loan from the hard money lender. By then, the hard money lender had already collected $650,000 and the business still owed $1.8 million. That's almost $2.5 million for the lender on a $1.2 million loan-with the 12% interest still ticking. Fortunately for Butch, the property was valuable enough that we were able to refinance and pay off this lender. But the transaction cost Big Land more than a million dollars, and *almost* cost them the entire property. Had Big Land gone to a traditional bank in the first place, the high value of the land would have enabled them to borrow the development funds at a cost of about $100,000 over two years, instead of $1.2 million.

Hard money lenders have their place. But you should only use them for short term loans to cover a specific, unusual need. They are not to be used to finance the normal operation of the business or for a partner buyout.

Investors

Taking on an investor is different from the other forms of financing. Investors come in two different forms, broadly described as Friends and Family, or Venture Capital/Private Equity. Investors can provide funds to buy out your old partner, but those investors will become your new partners.

Friends and Family

In the start-up phase, business partnerships often seek funding from people they know. They will invest because they believe in the partner, not because they truly understand the business. These investors will generally risk fairly small amounts, so you'll need lots of them to raise significant capital. A typical "F and F" round might raise $750,000 from 20 investors at $25,000 to $50,000 each.

A partnership can raise money from Friends and Family before its business model is proven, or at a time of transition, like buying out a partner. This has the advantage of getting you cash when you need it, but also the disadvantage of not putting your business model through the same rigors that a more sophisticated investor will require.

An F and F round also creates more partners for you to manage. This can be difficult. It seems there are always a few small investors who will demand to know every detail of your operation and will question every move you make. You can waste a lot of time explaining to your unsophisticated brother-in-law why it's beneficial to carry less inventory, even though inventory appears as an asset on the balance sheet.

If you raise money through Friends and Family, it's important to do so *formally*. These investors become your business partners, and you should take the same care in choosing them as you would with any new partner. Both sides need the protection of a *Private Offering Memorandum* disclosing the risks, and an *Accredited Investor Questionnaire*, so you know they can handle the risk. You will also need to update your *Operating Agreement* and *Control Agreement*, and have the investors sign these documents.

Venture Capital/Private Equity

Venture Capital and Private Equity firms are sophisticated investors. These firms will not simply lend money, they will want to *buy* a piece of the business. If the business is successful, this can be very expensive. They own a piece of the business, so they will take a percentage of profits over the years, and eventually a percentage of the sale price of the business. Investment firms are always looking for bargains, and are always tough negotiators. They expect a return of 15 to 20 *times* their initial investment.

162

The upside of these firms is that it's a good way to mitigate the owner's risk. Often, venture capital can provide enough money to give the owner the double win of obtaining financial security while allowing her to buy out her partner.

It's important to keep in mind that the VC firm will become your new business partner. As discussed in the previous chapters, you must choose your partners carefully. Venture Capital firms have different requirements. Some will just let you run your business your way, as long as you hit your numbers. Some firms are very intrusive, placing tight controls over your business decision making. My client William was forced to give up his company car (a Mercedes Benz) and drive a less expensive car, because the investors wanted to cut expenses.

Venture Capital and Private Equity firms can provide the capital and expertise you need to accelerate growth. If it works out, you will give them a lot of money in the end, but you will also get to keep a lot for yourself.

The Rest of the Story

Dan's situation looked bleak. Depending on the length of the pandemic, the company faced defaulting on their bank loans, losing key employees, and damaging their supplier relationships. In the long term, bankruptcy might be inevitable. However, Dan wanted to take advantage of the opportunity to buy Lee's shares.

The first problem was keeping his employees. He had trained his team well and didn't want to lose any of them. Dan was able to secure a loan through the Federal Paycheck Protection Program. Through this program, Dan was able to keep his employees, even though they were not producing anything. This loan was eventually forgiven at the end of the program.

Dan still needed money to pay his other bills, and to buy Lee's shares. Dan's capital solution, ironically, was in the size of his bank debt. The bank needed its $4.5 million loan to perform. The bank knew the business well. Because the bank believed in the business, they were willing to support it with *more* financing and, importantly, more *time*. We were able to convince the bank to defer payments for three months, then accept interest only for another three months. The bank also agreed to lend another $900,000, secured by the excess inventory, turning that problem into a benefit. This gave Dan the time and capital he needed to get through the non-revenue period and buy Lee's shares.

About the Author

Bring Your Bulldog

Terry earned his reputation as a "bulldog lawyer" by being aggressive, tenacious, and practical. He has successfully taken on major league adversaries including big oil, big pharma, and big government, in both litigation and transactions. Over the past 30 years, he has won more than $150 million for his clients.

He's especially good at handling business partner disputes. He's the author of two books, *Big Force Negotiation*, and *The Bulldog Guide to Business Divorce*.

Terry advises business clients in a variety of sectors, with concentrations in oilfield services, media, sports, health care, and real estate.

Terry has owned and operated successful radio properties, a summer league for pro hockey players, and a real estate investment company. This unique experience, in both law and business, gives him the specialized skills to solve disruptive business problems, from litigation to transactions to multi-party workouts.

Terry is licensed to practice in Minnesota and North Dakota. He's also a popular speaker and seminar leader on business issues. To listen to his weekly podcast, "Moore About the World," browse to https://www.mooreabouttheworld.com/podcast

If you have concerns about your business partnership, we can help.

If you have questions, or would like to arrange for Terry to speak to you group, contact him directly at 612-396-5588.

Terrance W. Moore, Esq.

Helmuth & Johnson
8050 W 78th Street
Edina, MN 55439
www.GuideToBusinessDivorce.com

TMoore@HJLawFirm.com

Made in the USA
Monee, IL
13 January 2022

88867319R00105